'In this highly engaging exploration of the letter to the Roman churches, Andrew Ollerton's natural and communicative style provides readers with an accessible account of the ancient truths in this magisterial letter.'

Dr Lucy Peppiatt, author and
Principal, WTC Theology

'Fresh, succinct, simple, yet with depth and insight, this survey of Romans will be invaluable to new as well as seasoned readers of this most important letter of Paul.'

Rev Charles Price, author and pastor,
The Peoples Church, Toronto

'St Paul's Romans is one of the most important books of the Bible, but not the easiest. Andrew Ollerton has a gift for not only communicating it accessibly but also showing its deep and practical relevance to life now.'

David F. Ford, Emeritus Regius Professor
of Divinity, University of Cambridge

'Andrew's book has been both a welcomed education and inspiration. It has given me greater understanding and confidence of the pivotal place of Romans in our discipleship and mission. I believe it is a must-read for anyone wanting to better equip themselves in understanding, and believing, why we should not be "ashamed of the gospel, because it is the power of God that brings salvation to everyone who believes" . . . I love it!'

Rev Mark Greenwood, National Evangelist and
Head of Evangelism, Elim Churches UK

T0299575

'A practical and rich companion to help you journey through the book of Romans. Deep theology sits wonderfully alongside incredibly relatable illustrations in this powerful, challenging and hopeful book.'

Gavin Calver, CEO, Evangelical Alliance

'Romans is one of the great masterpieces of Scripture, and Dr Ollerton offers us an introduction to that masterpiece with the language, questions and ideas of our world. His clear analogies, engaging communication and practical questions create an invitation to read this Gospel letter with confidence.'

Canon Sarah Yardley, Mission Lead, Creation Fest UK

'A grasp of the truth of Paul's epistle to the Romans is utterly life changing, yet so many believers are happier sticking to the gospels or the psalms. Andrew Ollerton's book is such an attractive, approachable invitation to modern believers to plumb its depths and ascend its heights.'

Terry Virgo, founder of Newfrontiers

'Every Christian needs to have a grasp of Paul's letter to the Romans. You will find no wiser guide to this earthshaking letter than this accessible and helpful book which navigates every difficulty with both ease and enthusiasm. Recommended!'

Rev Canon J. John

'Andrew manages to take the Scripture and make it relevant to today's audience. A blend of the serious and humorous, masterly conveyed in its original context.'

Pastor Mick Fleming, author of *Blown Away*

'This book unravels the good news of the gospel: that hope, freedom and salvation can emphatically impact and change those who encounter and receive it. The heart of God connects with the lost, abandoned and broken in society, who in turn are sent with the same transforming message.'

Nigel Langford, Bible Society

'This is an enlightening and engaging guide to the highest peak in the mountain range of New Testament letters. Andrew Ollerton makes difficult paths seem easy as he takes us on this tour. We get insights into the cultural setting of the Bible, as well as how we should apply it to life today.'

Dr Peter Williams, Principal, Tyndale House

'Andrew's historical insights and storytelling make it a great resource for small groups and I will be journeying through it again with friends. Ultimately, this book is a valuable reminder of the reality of the Gospel.'

Andy Frost, Share Jesus International

'Romans is the Himalayas of the Bible and Andrew Ollerton is your sure-footed guide. Read this one slowly, and with your Bible open; it will do you so much good.'

Glen Scrivener, author of *The Air We Breathe*

'Have you ever attempted to read, let alone understand Romans? Andrew Ollerton is determined to make Romans accessible to the normal Christian. Key truths are stated, explained, illustrated and applied. The church owes Andrew a huge debt for opening up this glorious letter.'

Rico Tice, co-founder of Christianity Explored

'There is perhaps no more urgent task for today's church than to re-engage Christians with the story of Scripture, and Andrew Ollerton has a wonderful gift of doing just that. Read this book and you will re-discover the riches of the gospel and the grandeur of the story we are all invited to be part of.'

Justin Brierley, Apologetics and Theology editor, Premier

'Rather than shying away from the daunting mountain that is Romans, Andrew Ollerton takes it on, and takes the reader too on an adventure through its heights and depths. With inimitable pace and energy, the book explores the sometimes challenging, but ultimately hope-filled truths that Romans reveals, shining a light on its relevance for us today.'

Chine McDonald, author, broadcaster and director of Theos

'There are parts of the Bible and Christian life that look like massive mountains we would love to climb but just seem to defeat us quickly. Andrew Ollerton does the job of an expert mountain guide helping you to understand, enjoy and apply Romans to your Christian life. It is an adventure that Christians, young and old, will treasure and then lead others on the same path.'

Jonathan Thomas, pastor, author and BBC broadcaster

'You don't have to be a Christian to read this book! When I read St Paul's letter to the Romans in a hotel room in 1986 I was not a Christian, but when I had finished reading it I felt compelled to become one! Having read Andrew Ollerton's most wonderful 'guide' book, I have been able to revisit this extraordinary letter in such a new and refreshing way. On all my travels, if all I had in my bag were the four Gospels, Paul's letter to the Romans and Andrew Ollerton's book, I would be tempted to feel that I would need nothing else!'

Sir David Suchet, actor

ROMANS

A Letter That Makes Sense of Life

ANDREW OLLERTON

HODDER &
STOUGHTON

First published in Great Britain in 2023 by Hodder & Stoughton
An Hachette UK company

8

Copyright © Andrew Ollerton, 2023

The right of Andrew Ollerton to be identified as the Author of the Work has been asserted by him in accordance with the Copyright, Designs and Patents Act 1988.

Unless indicated otherwise, Scripture quotations are taken from the *Holy Bible, New International Version (Anglicised edition)*. Copyright © 1979, 1984, 2011 by Biblica Inc.® Used by permission. All rights reserved.

Scripture quotations marked MSG are taken from *The Message*, copyright © 1993, 2002, 2018 by Eugene H. Peterson. Used by permission of NavPress. All rights reserved. Represented by Tyndale House Publishers, Inc.

Scripture quotations marked ESV UK are taken from *The Holy Bible, English Standard Version*® (ESV®), copyright 2001 by Crossway Bibles, a publishing ministry of Good News Publishers. Used by permission. All rights reserved.

Scripture quotations marked NKJV™ are taken from the *New King James Version*®. Copyright © 1982 by Thomas Nelson, Inc. Used by permission. All rights reserved.

Scripture quotations marked NLT are from *The Holy Bible New Living Translation*, copyright © 1996, 2004, 2007 by Tyndale House Foundation. Used by permissions of Tyndale House Publishers, Inc., Carol Stream, Illinois 60188. All rights reserved.

Scripture quotations marked J. B. Phillips are taken from *The New Testament in Modern English by J.B Phillips* copyright © 1960, 1972 J. B. Phillips. Administered by The Archbishops' Council of the Church of England. Used by Permission.

Image of Harriet Tubman on page 211: Alpha Historica / Alamy Stock Photo

All rights reserved. No part of this publication may be reproduced, stored in a retrieval system, or transmitted, in any form or by any means without the prior written permission of the publisher, nor be otherwise circulated in any form of binding or cover other than that in which it is published and without a similar condition being imposed on the subsequent purchaser.

A CIP catalogue record for this title is available from the British Library

Trade Paperback ISBN 978 1 399 80642 8
eBook ISBN 978 1 399 80644 2

Typeset in Ehrhardt by Hewer Text UK Ltd, Edinburgh
Printed and bound in Great Britain by Clays Ltd, Elcograf S.p.A.

Hodder & Stoughton policy is to use papers that are natural, renewable and recyclable products and made from wood grown in sustainable forests. The logging and manufacturing processes are expected to conform to the environmental regulations of the country of origin.

Hodder & Stoughton Ltd
Carmelite House
50 Victoria Embankment
London EC4Y 0DZ

www.hodderfaith.com

Contents

Acknowledgements

It takes many friends to write a book. Lots of generous people have carved out time to read, revise and endorse this piece of writing. I'm particularly grateful to Rev Howard Peskett, Prof John Coffey, Prof David Ford and Dr Lucy Pepiatt. Their scholarly insights significantly sharpened earlier drafts. The team at Hodder, along with my colleagues at Bible Society, have kept me going with their ideas and enthusiasm. Thank you! I also owe a debt of gratitude to former students and church members who scrambled with me through earlier approaches to Romans and encouraged me to share it more widely. Finally, I wish to dedicate this book to my adventurous family. A few years ago, we camped out on a Welsh mountain. Under the stars, I turned on my kindle and began to read the letter of Romans . . . what happened next inspired the book you are about to read.

PREFACE

Basecamp

*'It's a dangerous business, Frodo, going out your door. You step
onto the road, and if you don't keep your feet, there's no knowing
where you might be swept off to'*
J. R. R. Tolkien, *The Fellowship of the Ring*

Whenever we venture into wild places, our children know what's coming. The promise of a 'short walk' turns into an adventure – jumping in plunge pools, lighting fires, getting lost, foraging for food. They are plucky kids and we love exploring wild places together. One of my favourite memories is climbing a mountain called Skiddaw in Northern England. The original plan was to stroll up a foothill, aptly named Little Dodd. But our kids decided to head straight up the main mountain, which they renamed 'Everest'. It's amazing what children can do when it's their idea, isn't it? Fuelled by wild blueberries, gorse blossom (you can eat the yellow flowers) and water from a stream, we reached the summit and enjoyed spectacular views over the Lake District. Not bad considering they were three and five at the time!

For as long as I can remember, high places have been my happy place, where I find physical and emotional refreshment.

However, what you may not fully appreciate is that mountains hold spiritual significance too. Think about some dramatic stories in the Bible – the testing of Abraham and Isaac on Mount Moriah, the giving of the Law to Moses on Mount Sinai, Elijah taking on the prophets of Baal on Mount Carmel, the glory of Jesus revealed on the Mount of Transfiguration. Why did these iconic events take place at altitude? Perhaps the imposing nature of mountains demonstrates the distance between us and God? Or maybe the elevation helps to convey the scale of what's unfolding? We can't be certain.

However, one thing is clear. God often meets people in the great outdoors. Some of my most profound spiritual experiences have been while exploring rugged landscapes. Woodlands, lakes, mountains, coastline, moorlands. These are nature's cathedrals that call forth praise to the Almighty. In wild places, my soul is tamed and God draws near.

Recently, our family camped on a mountain in the Brecon Beacons. Once the children were asleep, I started reading the New Testament letter to the Romans on my Kindle. I couldn't put it down. It revealed truths more majestic than the Milky Way that twinkled overhead. When I reached chapter 8, I became overawed by the sheer scale of God's purpose: 'creation itself will be liberated . . . and brought into the freedom and glory of the children of God' (8:21). As I sat by the campfire, I felt my heart strangely warmed by famous promises: 'in all things God works for the good of those who love him . . . [nothing] will be able to separate us from the love of God that is in Christ Jesus our Lord' (8:28, 39). Romans is an incredible letter. No matter how many times I've read it, like a rugged landscape, it keeps revealing hidden vistas.

Inspired by my experience that night, I decided to write the book you are now reading.

PAUL'S LETTER TO ROME IS THE HIGH PEAK OF
SCRIPTURE . . . ALL ROADS IN THE BIBLE LEAD
TO ROMANS, AND ALL VIEWS AFFORDED BY THE
BIBLE ARE SEEN MOST CLEARLY FROM ROMANS.

J. I. Packer[1]

It's been said that if the New Testament were the Himalayas,
Romans would be Mount Everest and chapter 8 would be the
summit. Given my love of mountains, I couldn't resist drawing
on this metaphor. Let's try to imagine Romans as a vast landscape – complex and challenging but highly rewarding.
Together, we will take on the challenge of ascending to the
summit, enjoying the view and then descending to put into
practice what we've learned on the other side.[2] However, if you
are afraid of heights or prefer the great *indoors*, don't worry –
the mountain metaphor is just a visual aid to help us navigate
Romans. Muddy boots and blisters are optional!

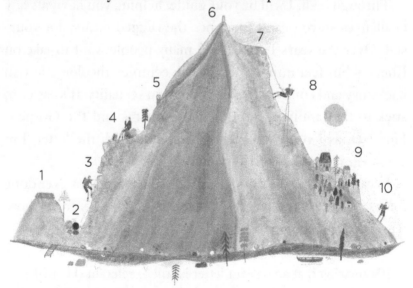

1 THE ROUTE OF THE GOSPEL **2** THE VALLEY OF SIN **3** THE CRUX OF SALVATION
4 THE PLACE OF PEACE **5** THE RIDGE OF FREEDOM **6** THE SUMMIT OF HOPE
7 THE CLOUD OF MYSTERY **8** THE DESCENT OF DEVOTION
9 THE RETURN TO COMMUNITY **10** THE ONWARD MISSION

This image captures the adventure that lies ahead. First, we will consider the original context of the letter and survey *the route of the gospel*. Then we must head down into *the valley of sin*, a low point from which we need rescuing. *The crux of salvation* reveals how Jesus has secured the way out, by faith. This brings us to *the place of peace*, where we take a breather and bask in the love of God. Then we will press on up *the ridge of freedom* – a narrow section with steep drops on either side. Suddenly, we will emerge onto *the summit of hope* and enjoy panoramic views of God's eternal purpose. Next we must navigate *the cloud of mystery*. Here it's easy to feel lost as we consider why God chose Israel and whether he still has a special purpose for them? Finally, then we head down into more practical teaching. *The descent of devotion* calls us to a life of radical love, and *the return to community* shows us how to make a difference in society. *The onward mission* will equip us to share the good news with others.

Through it all, I will be your guide, helping you navigate any challenges so you can experience the rugged beauty for yourself. Over the years I've realised many people want to take on Romans but feel intimidated by the complex theology, Jewish backstory and controversial teachings on sexuality. It's easier to stick to the familiar foothills of the Psalms and the Gospels. However, as I've led groups of people through the letter, I'm always impressed by the impact it makes.

In case you are still wondering, 'What has Romans ever done for us?' (cue John Cleese), here are some reviews from those who have gone before you:

> It's amazing that an ancient letter is still so relevant (Hannah)
> I experienced God's love in a personal way (Alice)
> The whole Bible makes more sense (Danny)
> Romans gave me a new perspective on life (Simon)

As with any great adventure, the effort you put in is more than rewarded by the experiences you gain along the way. So don't be put off by the scale of the challenge. These chapters will guide you each step of the way. And just think . . . once you've conquered Romans, the whole Bible will be easier to explore.

Each chapter of this book is divided into two parts and follows a similar pattern. First, we *Look At* Romans to see what each passage meant in its original context. Then we *Look Through* Romans – as if through a lens – to see what it means today. This double movement ensures we do justice to the biblical text, allowing it to speak on its own terms. After all, the letter was not written in the twenty-first century. Ancient Rome was a very different society: rife with human trafficking and slavery, narrow streets with no refuse collection, blood sports in the arena and new-born babies discarded on rubbish heaps.

> ROMAN HISTORY DEMANDS A PARTICULAR
> SORT OF IMAGINATION . . . IT SEEMS
> COMPLETELY ALIEN TERRITORY.
> Mary Beard[3]

The more we understand Romans within the cultural context in which it was written, the richer the meaning will become. For example, the instruction, 'Greet one another with a holy kiss' (Rom. 16:16) sounds odd for those of us who are used to a culture of hugs and handshakes. But in the first century it was a sign of true acceptance. Imagine a wealthy Christian master being instructed to greet his slave with this sign of honour and respect! Customs and instructions that sound quirky to us were revolutionary for them.

It is also important to *look through* Romans. Imagine the letter like a pair of spectacles to wear. You don't so much look at them as through them. They focus your whole vision. Romans is not just a piece of ancient correspondence; it is a pair of lenses that God has provided. We are by nature short-sighted about the future and prone to missing the point. But Romans is a letter that restores our vision and helps us make sense of life.

> ROMANS IS ABOUT THEOLOGY, BUT
> IT ISN'T MERE THEOLOGY – IT ISN'T
> ABSTRACT THEOLOGY. IF YOU WILL, THE
> THEOLOGY OF ROMANS IS ABOUT A WAY
> OF LIFE, ABOUT LIVED THEOLOGY.
> Scot McKnight[4]

In my experience, Romans has the wisdom we need to flourish in an ever-changing world. So make sure you explore the letter itself alongside this book. At the beginning and halfway through each chapter there are suggested passages to read from Romans. Complete these, and you will have read the whole letter. There are also reflection points within each chapter to help process what we are learning.

For me, an adventure is more enjoyable in the company of others. So why not invite some friends to join in so you can read and discuss together along the way?

Finally, before we leave basecamp, take a moment to gather the kit you will need – a modern translation of Romans (I will be using the NIV UK, 2011 edition[5]), a notebook to jot down any thoughts, and a sense of humour for when it gets challenging!

When you are ready, pull on your boots and let's get going . . .

The route of the gospel

Romans 1:1–17; 16:1–27

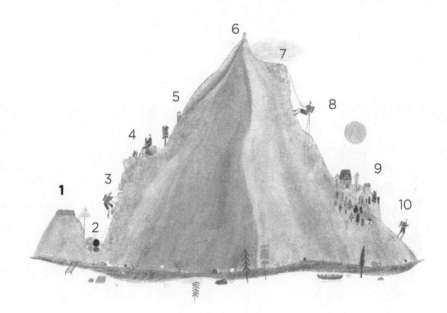

Political prisoners were assigned the worst and most miserable chores in this particular jail. For Hien, that meant cleaning out the guards' latrine. The prisoner retched as he reached in with bare hands. Suddenly, he spotted a scrap of paper with writing in a foreign language. Pulling it out, he slipped it into his pocket and continued with the task.

Later that night, back in his cell, he cleaned off the remaining excrement and began to read. Now, bear in mind that the night before, Hien Pham had decided to give up on God altogether. Having been raised a devout Buddhist in Vietnam, he had become a Christian in the 1970s when an American soldier gave him a Bible during the war. Hien then served as a translator for American missionaries. But when they left, the Communists turned on him and after months of beatings and brainwashing, it seemed they had finally broken him . . . until he stumbled on a scrap of Romans, which the prison guard had 'used' earlier that day. As Hien read these words, he began to weep:

> And we know that in all things God works for the good of those who love him, who have been called according to his purpose . . .

> Who shall separate us from the love of Christ? Shall trouble or hardship or persecution or famine or nakedness or danger or sword? . . . No, in all these things we are more than conquerors through him who loved us.
>
> *Romans 8:28, 35, 37*

That night, Hien decided not to give up on God, since God had clearly not given up on him. The next day, he volunteered to clean out the latrine again. Fortunately, the prison must have been short on toilet paper and the guards continued to use pages torn from a confiscated Bible instead. Each day, Hien discovered another sheet of truth, deposited in the most unlikely place.[1]

Even just a scrap of Romans ripped out of context can change everything. That's how powerful it is. The mighty Roman Empire may now be confined to the history books, but this letter, written to Christians in ancient Rome (*c.* AD 55), continues to transform lives. In fact, there's a long list of famous people down the centuries for whom Romans has been revolutionary – St Augustine (fourth century), Martin Luther (sixteenth century), John Wesley (eighteenth century), Karl Barth (twentieth century). More recently, Sir David Suchet (otherwise known as Hercule Poirot) became a Christian when he read Romans in a hotel room.

The letter was originally written to ordinary people facing tough circumstances, like Hien Pham. Romans doesn't belong to scholars, though they can help us. Instead, it conveys in plain terms such great news that those who read it may never be the same again.

In this chapter, we begin our approach by surveying the landscape as a whole and familiarising ourselves with the route we must take. In particular, we will consider the opening section

(Rom. 1:1–17) along with the final greetings in Romans 16. These passages introduce the backstory and big themes of the letter and so provide a route map for all that is to come.

Without an accurate map, it's easy to lose your way and become lost. On a misty mountain in Scotland, my father and I once stumbled across a man who looked relieved to see us. He admitted he was lost and did not have a map to find his way. In fact, he was so disorientated he had set off up a different mountain from the one he was supposed to be climbing! It was a timely reminder to study the route map before charging off into the unknown. If we pay close attention to the opening and closing sections of Romans, they will provide the map we need to stay on track throughout the adventure.

Part 1: The backstory

By beginning with the personal greetings in Romans 16, we will discover the original context and how its radical message challenged social hierarchies in ancient Rome.

Part 2: The big themes

Paul was confident in the truth of the gospel, despite all the luxuries and glamour of ancient Rome. How can we become more confident in the gospel today?

> I am not ashamed of the gospel, because it is the power of God that brings salvation to everyone who believes.
>
> *Romans 1:16*

Part 1: The backstory

READ: Romans 16:1–24

The letter to the Romans adopts the standard format of most letters in the ancient world. Unlike our correspondence, which states the name of the recipient upfront ('Dear Aunty Edna . . .'), Romans works the other way around. It begins by introducing the author and their reasons for writing (Rom. 1:1–17), then there are the main contents of the letter organised into four sections (chapters 1—4, 5—8, 9—11, 12—15). Only at the end do we discover who it was originally addressed to. Chapter 16 greets twenty-seven people by name. From these bookend sections we can piece together the backstory of Romans.

Who wrote Romans?

The answer to this question may seem obvious: the Apostle Paul, right? Well, yes and no. Take a look at Romans 16:22: 'I *Tertius*, who wrote this letter, greet you in the Lord' (ESV UK, italics added). However, Romans 1:1 does indeed say that the letter is from 'Paul'. So what's going on?

In the ancient world, before printers and computers, you could employ a professional scribe (known as an *amanuensis*) to write important documents. In Paul's case this was not because he was illiterate, but he may have had a severe eye condition that affected his ability to write neatly (see Galatians 6:11). So the words and ideas in Romans came straight from Paul, but Tertius was the scribe who put pen to paper. The poor chap deserves a medal for keeping up with the great Apostle and capturing such complex ideas!

The relationship between Paul and Tertius illustrates a more general point about the authorship of the Bible. While Paul didn't put pen to paper, he was the originator of Romans in the sense that the ideas stemmed from him. In the same way, God didn't put pen to paper, yet he is the ultimate author of the Bible. He inspired the ideas that humans wrote in such a way that the Bible is God's trustworthy truth. As Paul concluded in another letter, 'All Scripture is God-breathed' (2 Tim. 3:16).

This is important to remember as we read Romans. The *author* of a text gives it *authority*. If we imagine Romans to be merely the ancient musings of a first-century person who thought the earth was flat, then we may be tempted to dismiss it – especially the challenging bits. However, if Romans is ultimately a letter inspired by God, then we should want to embrace its message. Through a unique encounter with the risen Jesus, Paul was given special authority to write Scripture. The message of Romans is therefore far more than human ideas or suggestions. So, let's embrace it and take it to heart – even the challenging bits!

Who was Paul?

The way Paul introduces himself at the start of the letter would have been a shock: 'Paul, a servant of Christ Jesus' (1:1). Romans was originally written in Greek, and the first two words rhymed: *Paulos doulos*. The word *doulos* literally means 'slave'. In the first century, it is estimated that more than 30 per cent of the population of Rome were the property of wealthy masters. Treated much like machines, slaves could be bought, sold and, if necessary, beaten. If you were unfortunate enough to be born a slave, your goal was to become a *freed man* – someone released to be his or her own boss. That's why the opening verse of Romans is so bizarre. Paul was a well-educated Roman citizen from a prestigious background. In a culture where every slave wanted to be free, this free man proudly identified as a 'slave of Christ Jesus'.

This subversive introduction reveals how much Paul was obsessed with Jesus Christ. Like an annoying friend who's met the girl or boy of their dreams and won't shut up about them, from the moment Paul encountered Jesus on the Damascus Road he became Paul's 'magnificent obsession'.[2] Unsurprisingly, the most frequent words in Romans are 'God' (x153) and 'Jesus' or 'Christ' (x65). Previously, Paul was known as Saul. And Saul was a religious zealot who hated Christians – he even had a hand in murdering some (see Acts 22:4). But after a 180-degree turn and a name-change, Paul became the most influential Christian missionary of all time. The letter to the Romans captures the essence of the good news that left Paul blinded by grace (cue Stormzy[3]).

After following Jesus for many years, Paul became convinced that to discover true freedom involved embracing a counter-intuitive lifestyle as a servant of Jesus Christ. We will unpack this idea in more detail later in Romans, but for now, simply note the paradox – Jesus is the master who brings perfect freedom. For Paul, you are only truly free when you die to yourself and live for Christ. You will only discover your true self when you centre your whole life on God. Romans shows us how liberating life can be when Jesus becomes our 'magnificent obsession'.

JESUS OF NAZARETH . . . MAKES IT CLEAR THAT
GENUINE HUMAN HAPPINESS AND SATISFACTION
LIE MORE IN GIVING THAN RECEIVING; MORE
IN SERVING THAN IN BEING SERVED.
Queen Elizabeth II[4]

Who was Romans written to?

Christianity reached Rome without the direct influence of Paul. Perhaps it came through the Apostle Peter, or more likely merchants who first heard the good news in Jerusalem on the day of Pentecost and brought the message to Rome. Either way, by the time Paul wrote his letter, a substantial number of people were already meeting in several locations across town – perhaps as many as two hundred Christians. At the end of the letter, Paul mentions twenty-seven of them by name. In fact, Romans 16 contains more personal greetings than the rest of Paul's letters combined. Perhaps he wanted to show how relationally connected he was? Or maybe he mentioned key individuals from different groups to show that his message was for everyone? Whatever the reason, these personal greetings are a window into the early Christian community in Rome. Before we study some theology it's important to grasp their humanity. These were real people.

As I've examined Paul's greetings, two features really stand out. First, the early Christians were *deeply relational*. The Apostle Paul is often caricatured as stern, austere and even controlling. Romans 16 says think again. In an era before social media, the sheer number of personal names mentioned is impressive. It's like a holy network of relational connectivity. But what's even more striking is Paul's affectionate tone:

- verse 3: 'Greet Priscilla and Aquila . . . They risked their lives for me.' Paul uses a colloquialism here for execution: literally, 'They laid down their necks.' We might say, 'They took a bullet for me.'
- verse 9: 'Greet . . . my dear friend Stachys.' Someone we otherwise know nothing about is considered by Paul to be his 'beloved' or 'favourite' friend.

- verse 13: 'Greet Rufus . . . and his mother, who has been a mother to me, too.' What a remarkable way to refer to your friend's mum! It was as though she adopted Paul into her own family.

Paul's affection for these Roman Christians is obvious, but so is the depth of their loyalty to each other. They were a spiritual family risking their lives to serve Christ together. In a hostile context, they met secretively in small underground cells. That's why Paul greets not only individuals like Priscilla and Aquila but also 'the church that meets at their house' (16:5). Scholars estimate at least five distinct house churches gathered across the city. They didn't have the luxury of meeting in big buildings, nor was it safe to do so. Instead, some groups met in the villas of wealthy hosts while others may have gathered after hours in workshops or sheds.

As we imagine these ordinary people meeting to consider Paul's letter together, don't assume it was like a traditional church. Instead, imagine families and friends gathering with the doors locked, risking their safety. They were real people, tired from work, oppressed, hurting, yet hungry for the truth.

If, like me, you live in a safe context, it's important to remember that many brave Christians still risk their lives to meet together. Every morning over breakfast our family prays for one of the fifty most dangerous countries in the world to be a Christian. Today it was Burkina Faso, where a pastor and his son were recently murdered by Islamist extremists. That puts everything into perspective.

Second, the Roman Christians were *surprisingly diverse*. The list of names at the end of the letter reveals a remarkable range of people. There are Greek names (v. 14: Asyncritus, Phlegon, Hermes), Latin names (vv. 8–9, 15: Ampliatus, Urbanus, Julia) and Jewish names (vv. 3, 6–7: Aquila, Mary). Some were clearly wealthy masters who lived in a large villa or *domus* on one the famous seven hills that surrounded Rome. Aristobulus (v. 10) may even have been the grandson of Herod the Great. However, the majority would have been poor labourers living in squalid apartments along the shore of the River Tiber, which regularly flooded its banks.

Several of the names indicate that slaves were also part of the Christian community (e.g., Ampliatus, Asyncritus, Nereus). In a hierarchical society, where servants wiped their owners' backsides, it's revolutionary to have a list of greetings that makes no distinction between slaves and masters. Rich and poor, educated and illiterate may have been segregated in Roman society, but within the Christian community they ate at the same table and belonged to the same family.

> DIVERSITY SHAPED EVERY MOMENT OF
> THE ROMAN HOUSE CHURCHES, BUT PAUL
> SOUGHT FOR A UNITY IN THE DIVERSITY,
> A SIBLING RELATIONSHIP IN CHRIST THAT
> BOTH TRANSCENDED AND AFFIRMED ONE'S
> ETHNICITY, GENDER, AND STATUS.
> Scot McKnight[5]

Paul's greetings also allude to the significant role women played. Some have accused Paul of patriarchy or even misogyny. However, this seems unfair in the light of his references in Romans 16 to women who deserved public honour for their hard work and bravery (see verses 3–4, 6, 7, 12). In fact, according to an early Church father called John Chrysostom, 'the women of that time were more zealous than lions, sharing with the apostles in their labour of preaching'.[6]

In particular, a businesswoman may have been the first to publicly read and explain the letter of Romans to God's people: 'I commend to you our sister Phoebe, a deacon of the church in Cenchreae. I ask you to receive her in the Lord' (16:1–2).[7] Paul was probably in Corinth when he wrote Romans. Cenchreae is a nearby port. So Phoebe was given the task of taking one of the most important letters ever penned to Rome. Perhaps she was travelling there on business? This would have provided convenient cover as she secretly visited underground Christian cells across the city to share Paul's letter with them.

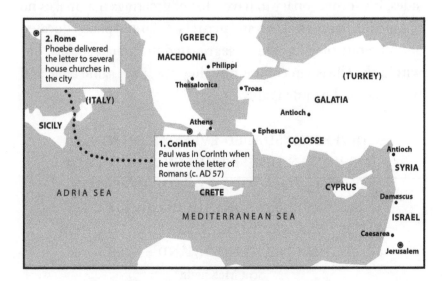

The journey of Paul's letter to Rome

Many scholars argue that Phoebe's role would not have been just to deliver the letter. In the ancient world, couriers were tasked with reading and, if necessary, further explaining the correspondence on behalf of the sender.[8] So in a culture dominated by men, imagine Phoebe reading Romans out loud to groups of poor workers and wealthy masters. Then questions would have been asked and further explanation given. Finally, copies would have been made so that each group could study the letter in more detail. By the way, it only takes the average reader an hour to read Romans in one sitting. Well worth doing before you move on to the next chapter, don't you think?

Phoebe remains a role model for all of us. We cannot write Scripture like the Apostle Paul, but we can follow in her footsteps. Imagine her reading the letter carefully on her way to Rome, perhaps memorising sections and reflecting on the tone and emphasis. By the time Phoebe arrived, she was ready to pass it on with passion and insight. That's our task too. We need to give Romans more than a cursory glance. Let's read, learn and inwardly digest it. Then we will be ready to share its transformative message with others.

> I KEEP HEARING [ROMANS] READ TWICE EVERY
> WEEK, AND OFTEN THREE OR FOUR TIMES . . .
> GLADLY DO I ENJOY THE SPIRITUAL TRUMPET,
> AND GET ROUSED AND WARMED WITH DESIRE
> AT RECOGNIZING THE VOICE SO DEAR TO ME.
> John Chrysostom (*c*.347–407)[9]

The remarkable diversity within the early Christian community – Jews and Gentiles, males and females, masters and slaves – was also a source of tension.[10] In fact, one of the themes that motivated Paul to write Romans was *unity* (another was *mission* – we'll get to that shortly). Paul only addresses these tensions directly towards the end of the letter (Romans 14—15). However, it's important to be aware of the issues up front as they inform the whole of Paul's argument. In particular, Paul was keen to build unity between Jews and Gentiles in the light of some recent events. Several years before Phoebe delivered Paul's letter to Rome, the Emperor Claudius had banished all

Jews from the city (see Acts 18:2). The Roman historian Suetonius gives a rather cryptic explanation as to why:

> Since the Jews constantly made disturbances at the instigation of Chrestus, he [the Emperor Claudius] expelled them from Rome.[11]

Most scholars assume 'Chrestus' refers to Jesus. Therefore, the disturbance that troubled Rome was between Jewish Christians and other Jews who opposed the idea that Jesus of Nazareth was Israel's Messiah. Either way, everyone else in the city would have concluded that Jews were troublemakers and Rome was better off without them. After Claudius' death in AD 54, Jews were allowed to return to the city. But can you imagine the tension? Gentile believers, who had got used to being the only Christians in town, now had to welcome back Jewish believers with their strange customs of circumcision, Sabbath laws and kosher foods. Mistrust soon developed. Perhaps they even doubted whether they were part of the same faith?

Today, when people from very different backgrounds, cultures and pay grades try to work together, it's easy for misunderstandings to arise and ghettos to form. There are clues that this was happening in Rome. In particular, some like Priscilla and Aquila had become Christians from a Jewish background. It was deeply engrained in them to keep certain holy days and to avoid certain foods. But other Gentile, or non-Jewish, Christians didn't have the same sensitivities – every day was a working day and any meat was good for the BBQ. With such differences in play, you can understand why things got tense. As we will see, Paul's goal throughout Romans is to demonstrate that 'in Christ' far more unites us than should ever divide us. The house churches across the city must not become suspicious of each other and splinter into Jewish cliques and Gentile denominations. Instead, the goal is that 'with one mind and one voice [we] may glorify the God and Father of our Lord Jesus Christ' (Rom. 15:6).

It is helpful to understand this backstory before we go any further. Now let's try to imagine the original scene . . . A family of poor Jewish believers enjoying a meal with some Roman slaves in a large villa on the outskirts of the city. A special guest has arrived with something to share. After dinner, curtains are drawn as she takes out a secret parchment from her shoulder bag. With hushed silence in the room, Phoebe begins to read:

> Paul, a servant of Christ Jesus, called to be an apostle and set apart for the gospel of God . . . To all in Rome who are loved by God and called to be his holy people:
>
> Grace and peace . . .
>
> *Romans 1:1, 7*

REFLECT: Imagine you are one of the Roman Christians meeting in a house church in secret. What might it have felt like to be there? Write down something that's inspired you about this early Christian community.

◯◯ Part 2: The big themes

READ: Romans 1:1–17

Having considered the backstory to Romans by *looking at* Paul's greetings (16:1–16), it's now time to *look through* Romans in order to grasp the relevance for today. The first half of chapter 1 (vv. 1–17) introduces the gospel, which the rest of the letter unpacks in detail. These verses therefore provide a vital route map for the rest of our adventure through Romans. If we pay attention to the big themes, it will enable us to follow the contours of Paul's argument and not stray off course. Personally, I have found these verses more and more inspiring as my understanding of the original context has deepened.

I wonder if there's somewhere you've always wanted to visit, a country or city? In the first century, the destination on everyone's bucket list would have been Rome. It was nicknamed the 'eternal city' by ancient poets. With more than a million residents by AD 100 it dwarfed all other urban centres. In fact, no other European city reached the equivalent population until London in the eighteenth century! The emperor, along with wealthy senators, lived in palatial luxury on the famous seven hills overlooking the city. They even enjoyed a heated swimming pool on the Esquiline hill (*c*.30 BC). As Roman armies defeated foreign enemies, thousands of captives were regularly paraded through the streets of Rome to display military might.[12] From AD 80 onwards, the spectacular Colosseum, a fifty- thousand-seat stadium for theatre and blood sports, dominated the skyline. Conquest and victory, power and glory were in the air. As historian Tom Holland put it, 'The Roman Empire put a premium on vanity!'[13]

I recently visited Rome myself to find out more about the city. Today, the famous Forum and Colosseum are part of a large archaeological site that preserves skeleton structures from the glory days.[14] Even these ruins convey a sense of grandeur that sends a shiver down your spine. That's why everyone longed to visit Rome, to admire the architecture and pay homage to the gods and celebrities who upheld it. Everyone, that is, except Paul. While most people dreamt of visiting Rome as tourists, Paul intended to go as an evangelist. His eagerness to visit was not because Rome had something Paul wanted but because Paul had a message that Rome needed:

I am eager to preach the gospel to you also who are in Rome.

For I am not ashamed of the gospel, for it is the power of God for salvation to everyone who believes.

Romans 1:15–16 (ESV UK)

In the first century, this was audacious confidence, bordering on arrogance. The eternal city seemed to have everything. What could a message about a crucified Jew have to offer Roman citizens with hot tubs, slaves and theatre tickets?

In this context, Paul's famous statement in verse 16 takes on added significance: 'I am not ashamed of the gospel'. The fact that he felt the need to say this indicates a certain amount of internal conflict. Paul knew what it was to feel intimidated, to question whether the simple message of Jesus was compelling enough for a culture with such glamorous alternatives. However, Paul also knew what it felt like to encounter the Messiah, risen from the dead. Now, after years of experience, he was convinced more than ever that Rome needed Jesus.

How confident are you that your city, colleagues, neighbourhood and friends need Jesus? Being honest, I struggle to see it sometimes. Unless a crisis flares up, my non-Christian friends seem pretty satisfied so long as their kids are safe, they holiday somewhere warm and their team isn't relegated. I wonder whether our rather polite and timid form of Western Christianity betrays an inner loss of confidence? Immersed in a culture with Premier League football, Netflix and Nando's, it's easier to live as cultural tourists. Perhaps, like me, you've felt awkward when Christianity comes up in conversation? So Romans chapter 1 begs the question: how confident are we in the power of the gospel today? Which would you circle for yourself?

1	2	3	4	5
PLAGUED BY DOUBT	VERY UNCERTAIN	UP & DOWN	MOSTLY CONFIDENT	FULLY ASSURED

Despite a lower score than I would like, studying Romans has moved my confidence further to the right. As I've immersed myself in Paul's arguments, I have become a bit bolder. Last night I went to the pub with friends I play football with. When they asked me what I do for a living, instead of side-stepping, I replied, 'I help people understand the Bible.' Awkward silence. Then one of them said he'd done Religious Studies A Level and remembered the Gospels.

'There's four of them, right?'

'That's right,' I replied, 'and that fact is enough to convince me.'

'What do you mean?'

'Well, in the ancient world, writing on parchments was expensive. Even a great Roman emperor would only deserve a couple of short biographies.'

'So?'

'For a Jewish carpenter, brutally crucified at a young age, to get four detailed biographies, something nuclear must have happened!'

Thoughtful silence. The conversation continues . . .

My hope as we journey through Romans is that we will all grow in confidence. For now, let me share a couple of reasons why Paul is not ashamed of the gospel from Romans 1:1–17.

Our enemies have been defeated by the risen Jesus (1:1–6)

The word 'gospel' sounds religious to us. But in the first century, the Greek word *euangelion* referred to an announcement of good news: *It's a girl! We won! I got the job!* If on a far-flung battlefield an emperor won a great victory, which secured peace and established his authority, he would send heralds or messengers to declare the good news of victory. The term 'gospel' therefore had political and social implications. Indeed, the rule of Emperor Augustus was referred to as the 'gospel' because he was the person who brought victory and established peace. The Empire had various propaganda machines – inscriptions on coins, imprints on pottery, images and statutes – which spread the message that the emperor was 'son of god' and 'lord' and 'saviour' of the Empire. In this cultural context, Romans 1:1–4 stands toe to toe with Caesar in proclaiming a new Lord, who is a very different kind of ruler:

> . . . the gospel he promised beforehand through his prophets in the Holy Scriptures regarding his Son, who as to his earthly life was a descendant of David, and who through the Spirit of holiness was appointed the Son of God in power by his resurrection from the dead: Jesus Christ our Lord.
>
> *Romans 1:2–4*

Notice in verse 2 that the gospel announcement is the fulfilment of a much larger story that is told throughout the rest of the Bible. In particular, the story centres on Israel as God's chosen people. In fact, the very structure of Romans echoes their plotline – including God's covenant with Abraham, the Exodus story and Israel entering the Promised Land.

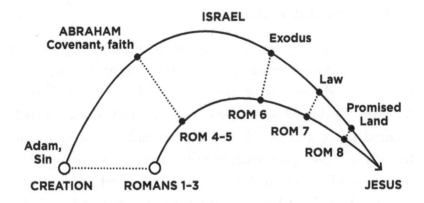

How Romans echoes the larger plotline of the Bible

The big idea of Romans is that Jesus the Messiah has fulfilled these ancient promises and released God's blessing to all nations. When God called Abraham, it was with a view to undoing the curses of Adam's disobedience (see Genesis 12). However, the Old Testament proves to be a puzzle because God's chosen family, Israel, become part of the problem they were meant to solve. The 'gospel of God' (Rom. 1:1) therefore announces the arrival of the one who can finally resolve the dilemma and thereby rescue our human race. The faithful ministry of Jesus, even to death on a cross, has broken the curse of sin and death and released God's blessing to all people. God's Spirit is now calling out a new humanity, the people of the Messiah, to bring hope to the world.

Perhaps you have heard the saying, 'all roads lead to Rome'? Roman engineers built a remarkable network of roads that spread out across the Empire. Someone in Briton, Gaul or Egypt only had to join their road and follow it for long enough and eventually they would end up in Rome.

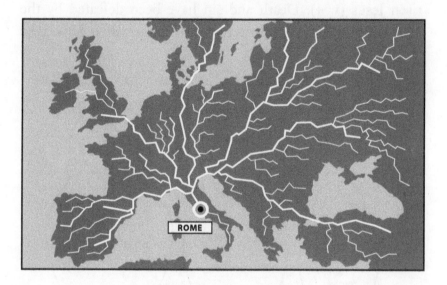

All roads lead to Rome

The way Paul interprets the Bible is like a system of Roman roads. Each character, symbol, story and event is part of a larger network of promises and prophecies, which are fulfilled in Jesus the Messiah. So the gospel message is not a new idea but something that was 'promised beforehand' (1:2).

With this in mind, Paul deliberately introduces Jesus as a 'descendant of David' (v. 3). King David was as close as Israel got to a Messiah in the Old Testament. He took down Goliath single-handed and brought peace to the nation. Now, Jesus has done for the world what David did

for Israel – singlehandedly defeating our enemies of sin and
death.

The most miserable and inevitable fact of life is that one in
one people dies. But the death and resurrection of Jesus are the
hinge upon which the story turns. Therefore, Paul's confidence
is not based on what we can do to change the world. The 'power'
of the gospel (v. 16) is drawn directly from the 'power' of the
risen Jesus (v. 4). Death and sin have been defeated by the
Messiah; new life and eternal hope are now on offer. This is the
'gospel of God' (v. 1).

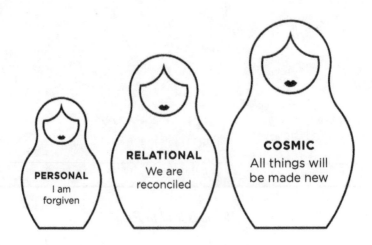

With this in mind, I find it helpful to imagine the gospel as a
set of nesting dolls. Though the gospel is one message – *Jesus
has won the victory over our enemies* – it can be applied on at
least three different levels. First, the victory of Jesus includes
personal salvation – forgiveness and freedom for the individual. Second, the gospel is good news at a *relational* level –
divisions are healed as Jew and Gentile, male and female,
black and white are united in Christ. Finally, the victory of
Jesus can be applied at a *cosmic* level. As Romans 8 makes

clear, the whole of creation is groaning for what lies ahead. So when you hear the word 'gospel', remember it's good news for you personally but also for governments, galaxies and everything in between.

> IF WE THINK THAT GOD'S POWER IS RESTRICTED
> TO THE SPHERE OF THE 'SPIRITUAL,' THEN
> WE HAVE A FAIRLY SMALL NOTION OF GOD.
> Beverly Gaventa[15]

Perhaps, like me, you enjoy watching Second World War films? My favourite used to be *Where Eagles Dare*, starring a young Clint Eastwood. I say 'used to be' because I recently watched it with my son and realised how dated the special effects were! Anyway, the reason we enjoy watching war films is because we already know the outcome. The allies won a decisive victory on D-Day, and the rest, as they say, is history.

For Paul, the gospel works like this. It is the announcement of a decisive victory that has already happened, right in the middle of history. Jesus' 'resurrection from the dead' (Rom. 1:4) means the outcome has already been secured. Our ultimate enemies – sin, evil and death – have been defeated, and there's no reversing what's already taken place. Jesus has been 'appointed the Son of God in power' (1:4). The day Jesus rose again was D-Day. He has been declared to be the true emperor, and the eternal city belongs to him! Now can you feel some of Paul's confidence? Now can you appreciate why both ancient Rome and our modern, sophisticated world need the good news of Jesus?

Through the 'righteousness of God', everyone is welcome (1:16–17)

Paul lived much of his life as a religious zealot. He had many reasons to take pride in his Jewish heritage and moral righteousness (see Philippians 3:1–11). Equally, he despised those he considered to be 'unclean sinners' – especially pagan Gentiles who had no share in Israel's privileges. However, his conversion involved a bizarre twist. Saul the great defender of exclusive Judaism became Paul the great missionary to non-Jews, or Gentiles. What underpinned this surprising new vocation was his deep conviction that God's good news is now for 'everyone who believes' (1:16). Paul explains why this is possible in verse 17: 'For in the gospel the righteousness of God is revealed – a righteousness that is by faith from first to last, just as it is written: "The righteous will live by faith."'

At the heart of the gospel is an important concept: 'the righteousness of God' (v. 17). This feature on the map is complex and several different routes have been proposed. Theologians debate whether 'the righteousness of God' refers to:

- **Route A. God's own righteous character**: God not only administers judgment for evil but, because he is faithful, he also provides salvation for Israel and the nations.
- **Route B. A gift of righteousness from God**: salvation means receiving righteousness as a gift so God no longer counts our sin against us but declares us to be justified.
- **Route C. Both of the above.**

In Romans 1:17, 'the righteousness of God' is in the possessive or genitive case. In other words, it describes something that belongs to God and not to us. So, in this verse Paul clearly has Route A in mind: the gospel reveals God's covenant faithfulness to Israel and the nations. However, when we come to unpack the inner workings of salvation, we will see that God's righteousness also leads to Route B: we are declared righteous as a gift (see Romans 4:11; 5:17). So we might conclude: Route A (God's righteous character) leads to Route B (our righteous status) which equals Route C.

If all this map work is making you feel nervous, don't panic. The key is that the gospel reveals God's saving action, which does not depend on our own moral standing or ethnic background. Jewish bloodline, Sabbath observance, foreskin removal – these no longer form the basis for who is 'in' or 'out'. Instead, God's righteous or faithful action through the gospel has brought salvation to 'everyone who believes'.

Think through the ramifications of this for today. Toxic forms of discrimination that plagued the first century seem to be making a comeback. But the gospel pulls the rug from under identity politics and culture wars. Regardless of ethnicity, race, gender or social background, everyone is welcomed into the same family through the righteousness of God. This gave Paul confidence as an evangelist. The message he shared was good news for every city. It may have begun in Jerusalem, but it belongs just as much in Rome, Barcelona and Beijing.

In verse 14 Paul therefore says, 'I am a debtor' under obligation to share the good news with 'Greeks and barbarians' (ESV UK). Paul imagines himself to be in debt to the people of Rome, though in a way we might not expect. If I were to borrow £1,000 from you, I would be in debt until I paid it back. But imagine someone gave me £1,000 to give to you. I would be just as much in debt until I passed on the gift.[16] In a similar way,

God has entrusted us with a good news message that is for everyone – whether sophisticated 'Greeks' or unschooled 'barbarians'. Paul's confidence to rock up to Rome was therefore based on these two convictions:

- Our enemies have been defeated by the risen Jesus.
- Through the righteousness of God, everyone is welcome.

As you consider these statements, perhaps you can feel your confidence levels rising? The gospel is really good news. There's nothing to be ashamed of. In the light of evil, suffering and death, everyone needs forgiveness and hope. Since Paul wrote Romans, we may have landed on the moon and invented the smartphone, but fundamentally our human condition remains the same, and so does the potency of this good news. The gospel *is* the power of God for salvation. It lifts people up, like it did Hien Pham; it can even transform whole communities. Theodoret, a Syrian bishop in the fifth century, likened the gospel to a spicy vegetable: 'A pepper outwardly seems to be cold . . . but the person who crunches it between the teeth experiences the sensation of burning fire.'[17] In the same way, as we bite into this ancient letter together, we will discover that the *power of God* is still working through the *gospel of God* today.

 REFLECT

1	2	3	4	5
PLAGUED BY DOUBT	VERY UNCERTAIN	UP & DOWN	MOSTLY CONFIDENT	FULLY ASSURED

In what ways has this chapter increased your confidence in the gospel? What honest doubts and fears still remain? Bring them to God and ask for his help.

I am not ashamed of the gospel, because it is the power of God that brings salvation to everyone who believes.

Romans 1:16

2
The valley of sin

Romans 1:18—3:20

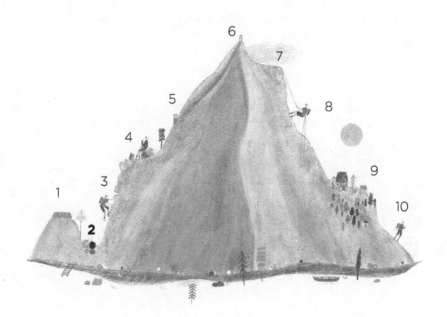

Who is that rude, arrogant driver using the wrong lane to skip the queue?
And why am I annoyed that I didn't think of it myself?

Who is 'Ashley' that just sent me a friend request (with semi-nude photo)?
And why am I tempted to click on it?

Who is responsible for all the dreadful violence and starvation in Yemen?
And why have I still not donated to the appeal that moved me?

We only have to turn on news channels or scroll social media to be reminded that there's something seriously wrong with the world. What's more revealing is the way we respond – indifference to those in need, envy of those succeeding, superficial judgments and subtle discriminations. There's something fundamentally flawed with me too. Romans 1:18—3:20 doesn't pull any punches regarding the broken state of the world and how God feels about it. However, these hard truths are not designed to harm us but to help us. After all, when we go to the doctor we need an honest diagnosis. Without this, we won't receive the right treatment. So, as part of getting ready to hear the good news, we need to first come to terms with some bad news.

Our ascent of Romans therefore begins with a surprise – we need to go down before we can start going up. I remember climbing one of my first big mountains in the French Alps. Before we began our ascent, we had to descend more than a thousand feet onto a glacier, which then led up towards the peak. It felt so hard to go down with the mountain already towering above us. But that was the only safe route. Likewise, the first three chapters of Romans lead us down into *the valley of sin* where we consider how low humans can go when we turn our backs on God. So take a deep breath. The first phase of a great adventure often feels hard.

As we saw in chapter one of this book, Romans was addressed to secret house churches scattered across Rome. A business-woman, Phoebe, was the courier and she probably read it out loud to each group, including wealthy patrons meeting in villas and poor workers in filthy sheds; Jewish Christians and ex-pagan Gentiles. The letter was designed to be read in one sitting, with each section forming part of the bigger picture. So what we are doing in this chapter isn't ideal. To isolate one section on sin from all that follows is like cutting a black patch out of a patchwork quilt and concluding that the whole thing is too dark. Remember, we are starting in *the valley of sin* where it can feel dark and threatening. But keep going and it will brighten up.

Part 1: What's wrong with the world?

In Romans 1 Paul grapples with the huge themes of creation, fall and judgment that echo back to the opening chapters of Genesis.

 Part 2: What's wrong with religion?

Paul then challenges those who are prone to judging others and warns them of judgment instead (Rom. 2). Just when all hope seems lost, we are ready for the gospel (Rom. 3:1–20).

> There is no difference . . . for all have sinned and fall short of the glory of God.
>
> *Romans 3:22–3*

Part 1: What's wrong with the world?

READ: Romans 1:18–32

The opening phrase of this passage sets up a deliberate contrast with where we left off. In 1:17 Paul declared that the gospel reveals 'the righteousness of God'. Remember, that phrase refers to God's faithful intervention to save his people. However, *gospel* or 'good news' implies that there is also some bad news. Paul introduces this in the next verse: 'The wrath of God is being revealed from heaven against all the godlessness and wickedness of people' (1:18).

The wrath of God implies his anger and judgment against evil. At the heart of this unpopular idea is a revelation of how God feels about the world he made and loves. So 'God's wrath' in the Bible should not be interpreted as something wild or unhinged. God is not a drunken father or tyrannical boss flying off the handle. He's angry and saddened because he cares about the damage caused by sin – whether personal, social or environmental.

Have you ever felt angry enough about an evil to roll your sleeves up and work to put it right? Imagine how William Wilberforce and the abolitionists must have felt about slavery in order to work tirelessly for half a century to see it ended. Likewise, God's wrath can be seen as an extension of his love – they are two inseparable sides of the same coin. God's judgment is therefore a vital theme that runs through the Bible story – from the original act of rebellion when God pronounced curses (Genesis) through to a future day of judgment (Revelation).

In Romans 1:18 Paul unpacks the wrath of God in a surprising way. He deliberately uses the present tense – God's wrath *is being revealed.* As well as affirming a final day of judgment (Rom. 2:5), Paul believes that God's wrath is in some sense already here. Divine judgment against sin is currently being felt in downtown Rome, leafy London suburbs and quaint Lake District villages. To explain this idea, Paul's argument takes the form of a downward slope:

CREATION v.18-20
God reveals himself
'Gods invisible qualities have been clearly seen'

SIN v.21-22
Humans reject God
'They exchanged the glory of God for images'

JUDGMENT v.24 ff.
God's wrath is revealed
'Therefore God gave them over in the sinful desires of their hearts'

Creation: God is revealed

Paul echoes Genesis by beginning with God's self-disclosure in the natural world: 'For since the creation of the world God's invisible qualities – his eternal power and divine nature – have been clearly seen, being understood from what has been made, so that people are without excuse' (1:20). Whether or not someone has heard the gospel, everyone can discern something of what God is like from the world around us. As an artist reveals their personality on canvas, so God displays his 'eternal power and divine nature' in creation. For example, NASA recently unveiled images of distant galaxies taken by the Webb Telescope, a successor to the Hubble Telescope. The depth and beauty of the images caught many off guard. Grown scientists broke down in tears as they took in the magnitude of what they were witnessing. Despite the rumours, the one who sustains these stars is not a miserable killjoy but an extravagant creator who delights in beauty and variety.

In addition to the natural environment, we have the witness of our moral conscience. If you were to ask someone, 'What's wrong with the world?,' all kinds of interesting answers would be given. But everyone, whether secular atheists or religious fundamentalists, acknowledges there is something wrong. As C. S. Lewis pointed out, to say a line is crooked implies there is a straight line.[1] To claim there are right and wrong ways to live implies there is a higher moral authority to which we are accountable.

Think about it, if ethics and morality are decided by majority vote, then slavery was not wrong in 1800 when most people were OK with it. In the TV programme *The Office*, David Brent (played by Ricky Gervais) recounts a racist name from a film about the Second World War. Having said the offensive word, he then covers his back by insisting that this was in the old days before racism was bad.[2] He's using comedy to put his finger on something profound.

Instinctively, we believe certain values are objective and therefore binding on all people at all times. Why do we feel this so deeply? In Romans, Paul argues we are hard-wired with a moral compass that points toward a higher standard. In summary, divine fingerprints are all over the natural world and God's eternal presence can be sensed by the human soul. Paul therefore considers the existence of God to be self-evident, so 'people are without excuse' (v. 20).

Sin: God is exchanged

I know 'sin' sounds like an old-fashioned word, but if you are a rugby fan like me you will know that it still has its uses.

What happens to a player who deliberately breaks the rules of the game? They are sent to the 'sin bin' for ten minutes. Rugby is such a Christian sport, don't you think? There are even several conversions during a match! Romans 1:21–3 traces what happens when humans *sin* by rejecting what they know deep down to be true. Three times Paul uses the word 'exchange' to capture it (vv. 23, 25, 26). Sin is not just being a bit naughty or disrespectful. At the heart of sin is replacing God with false substitutes known as idols. Here's how Paul puts it: 'Although they claimed to be wise, they became fools and exchanged the glory of the immortal God for images made to look like a mortal human being and birds and animals and reptiles' (1:22–3).

Ancient Rome was filled with temples that were landmarks across the city. Here priests would offer libations (liquid offerings) and sacrifices to various gods as part of mainstream culture. Think of these temples like spiritual banks where transactions took place: *If we sacrifice to the god of War (Mars) or Love (Venus) or the Sea (Neptune), they will give us military success or a baby or a safe crossing, or whatever.* In Romans 1, Paul squares up to this vast religious economy of sacrifices, rituals and rewards and declares the whole thing bankrupt: 'They *exchanged* the truth about God for a *lie*, and worshipped and served created things rather than the Creator' (1:25, italics added). The whole system was a fabrication based around superstition, bribery and debauchery. It was even thought the gods responded when their worshippers engaged in drunken orgies and ritual prostitution. How convenient! For Paul, these so-called gods were nothing more than social constructs, designer deities fashioned as substitutes for the real thing.

THE GODS WERE EVERYWHERE AND INVOLVED IN
EVERYTHING . . . THERE TO BE ACKNOWLEDGED,
APPEALED TO, PLEASED, OR PLACATED.
N. T. Wright[3]

However, that was first-century Rome. We don't worship idols today, do we?

I went to watch a football match with a friend recently. Before the game, we went to the pub for dinner. But I noticed my friend didn't order food, just plenty of drinks. Why not?

'I can't eat before a big game,' he told me, 'I get too nervous!'

The stadium was packed with fans chanting songs, wearing the kit, faces painted with their team's colours. When the players ran out, the fanatical crowd seemed to reach fever pitch. When our team scored a goal, the celebrations became frenzied. When the final whistle blew and our team had lost, the depression and anger were palpable. You'd be forgiven for thinking it was a matter of life and death but, as a former Liverpool manager Bill Shankly famously quipped, 'It's more important than that!' If an idol worshipper from first-century Rome had witnessed the spectacle, they might have felt strangely at home. A stadium-sized temple, where passionate fans fast and chant in an atmosphere charged with religious fervour.

Now, you may not be taken with football, but let's revisit the key verb in verse 25: 'they exchanged'. Whatever form it takes, our hearts are prone to replacing the true God with substitutes that promise more for less. So, the concept of idolatry should broaden our understanding of sin. It's not just doing *bad* things but putting *good* things in the place of God. In short, idolatry is worshipping anything that humans have made instead of worshipping the God who made humans.

We are hard-wired to worship. So if we reject the living God, we will find alternative shrines – shopping centres, offices, salons and gyms. As the French reformer John Calvin put it, the human heart is a 'perpetual idol factory'.[4] We make huge sacrifices in order to find *significance* and *security* in things we think we can control – careers, lovers, properties, sports, financial investments, body image, travel, academic achievements. All of these are *good*, but when we upgrade them to *god*, we cross the threshold of modern-day temples.

> THERE HAS TO BE SOMETHING WHICH IS THE
> RESTING PLACE OF OUR DEEPEST HOPES AND
> WHICH CAN CALM OUR DEEPEST FEARS . . .
> IT BECOMES OUR BOTTOM LINE, THE THING
> WE CANNOT LIVE WITHOUT, DEFINING
> AND VALIDATING EVERYTHING WE DO.
> Tim Keller[5]

According to Romans, idolatry is a symptom of a more basic rejection of God. Once you have something to hide, the presence of God becomes awkward, like a burglar bumping into a policeman. There is a deeper reason why people choose not to believe in God. It's not just about evidence; it's convenience. As the renowned philosophy professor Thomas Nagel admitted, 'It isn't just that I don't believe in God . . . It's that I hope there is no God! I don't want there to be a God; I don't want the universe to be like that.'[6] At the heart of sin are disordered desires that exchange God for other dreams, goals and lovers that promise to free us and fulfil us.

Judgment: God lets us go

Now comes the twist. Just when we might expect God to smite wicked sinners and stop them in their tracks, in fact he opens the door, gives them what they want and lets them go. Have you ever read the story of the prodigal son in chapter 15 of Luke's Gospel? The father gives the rebellious child his inheritance, much to the surprise of everyone else. For Paul, this is how the wrath of God is being worked out today. The key phrase is repeated three times and should send a shudder down your spine: '*God gave them over* in the sinful desires of their hearts . . .' (1:24, italics added).

> WHEN THE GODS WISH TO PUNISH
> US, THEY ANSWER OUR PRAYERS.
> Oscar Wilde[7]

In verse 26, Paul specifically notes that God 'gave them over to shameful lusts'. The Greek is *epithumia*, which literally means 'over-desire'. It's when you want something so much you become obsessed with it and controlled by it, going into overdrive to have it. In other words, it's addiction, it's bondage, it's being ruined by something you hoped would fulfil you. As David Foster Wallace has shown, when we worship idols we become enslaved by their dark side. Worship money and you will live in fear of never having enough. Worship body image or beauty and you will feel ugly and inadequate by comparison. Worship intellect and being smart and you will always feel like a fraud, on the verge of being found out. In short, apart from the living God, 'pretty much everything else will eat you alive'.[8] For Paul, the wrath of God is revealed when he removes his protective hand and allows these disordered desires to run away with us.

In Romans 1:24–7, Paul uses sexuality as a case study to illustrate his wider point about idolatry and the human condition.

CREATION
Sexual union is a
good gift for
husband and wife
to enjoy

SIN
We exchange the gift
for substitutes:
adultery, pornography,
impurity

JUDGMENT
Our disordered
desires lead
to lust, brokeness
and abuse

In the Bible, the story of creation affirms that sexual union is good. It is a divine gift to be enjoyed by husband and wife; making love and forming families. However, for those living in first-century Rome it was pretty obvious something had gone wrong. The whole city was founded on legends of sexual violence, including the famous 'Rape of Lucretia'. Orgies, brothels, cross-dressing, and pederasty (men sodomising boys) were commonplace. In AD 64, Emperor Nero hosted a summer festival in Rome where abuse was actively encouraged. For one night only, women were forbidden to refuse a man, whether slave or free.[9] Imagine the shame and hurt. This is what can happen when disordered desires are given full rein and humans swap the truth for a lie. The divine gift of sex is exchanged for dark lust, which leads to further brokenness.

*A Roman brothel coin from the second century AD: paying a prostitute
was socially acceptable for a free man in Rome*

In verse 26, Paul considers homosexual sex in order to illustrate
one way that he believes humans have departed from God's original purpose: '[they] exchanged natural sexual relations for
unnatural ones'. As a Jew, Paul considered the Old Testament to
be foundational. In Genesis, God created humanity male and
female, 'in his own image' (Gen. 1:27). This established a divine
pattern for procreation and sexual expression – namely that the
sexual act was intended to take place between a man and a woman
within the covenant of marriage. In light of this, the historic
understanding of the global Christian church has been that homosexual sex contradicts the divine pattern.[10] In recent years, this
issue has been hotly debated and is beyond the scope of this book.
However, it is important to note that the Bible nowhere condemns
a person for experiencing same-sex attraction. Indeed, Christian
theology makes an important distinction between *desire* and *action*
(see Jas. 1:13–14). Some Christian authors have reflected on their
experience of same-sex attraction and how they have chosen to
respond in the light of the teachings of Scripture. Their writings
provide a helpful way to consider these issues further.[11]

Romans 1 does not focus solely on sex, whether homosexual or heterosexual. Verses 29–31 list many other behaviours and attitudes that depart from God's pattern, including envy, gossip and disloyalty. Taken as a whole, Romans 1 is designed to highlight the ways in which we *all* fall short, regardless of religion, orientation or ethnicity. Paul would no doubt be appalled by the way some people have used certain verses to point the finger at others and deflect attention from themselves. The whole thrust of the argument is that no one is off the hook. Made in God's image, we are all called to faithfulness and purity. When we break promises, watch porn or gossip, we exchange the glory of God for idols that dehumanise us. The whole of society suffers when disordered desires run wild.

SEXUAL HOLINESS ISN'T JUST A 'RULE', AN ARBITRARY COMMANDMENT. IT IS PART OF WHAT IT MEANS TO TURN FROM IDOLS AND SERVE THE LIVING GOD. IT IS PART OF BEING A GENUINE, IMAGE-BEARING HUMAN BEING.

N. T. Wright[12]

To sum up this section of Romans, imagine a skilled craftsman fashioning a piece of maple wood into a violin. The wood has its own intricate pattern or grain that runs through the material. The craftsman must work with the wood; their tools must go with the grain. Only then will they fashion an instrument that can fill the room with music, dancing and joy. The world has been entrusted to us with a built-in pattern or grain. In the Bible, to go with the grain is to live with wisdom; to go against the pattern is folly. The world around us is not just a piece of plastic that we can mould any which way we please. We must go with the grain or our lives will become marred by splinters and brokenness. The message of Romans 1 may be hard to hear, but its challenge is designed to help us rediscover the way of human flourishing.

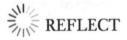 REFLECT

CREATION v.18–20
God reveals himself
'Gods invisible qualities have been clearly seen'

SIN v.21–22
Humans reject God
'They exchanged the glory of God for images'

JUDGMENT v.24 ff.
God's wrath is revealed
'Therefore God gave them over in the sinful desires of their hearts'

In what ways do we see this downward spiral in the culture around us? Write down some practical ideas for how you can work with the grain of God's pattern in your life.

◯─◯ Part 2: What's wrong with religion?

READ: Romans 2:1—3:20

Having *looked at* Romans 1:18–32, we must now *look through* Romans and consider how this teaching reframes our view of life. What different perspective do we get down in the *valley of sin*? As we'll see, becoming more aware of our true state can cultivate greater honesty, which is so good for us. However, first we should briefly reflect on what Paul does in Romans 2. Here he ensures no one can find a route that avoids *the valley of sin*. You see, it's possible for those of us who appear to live 'good' lives to look down on 'bad' people as if they belong in a different category. Of course, criminals, bullies, warmongers and Manchester City fans belong way down in the valley. But I'm a good person with higher standards, right? Surely I begin my ascent to God from a higher place?

While we might prefer to imagine humanity this way, Paul is determined to show that, before God, everyone is basically on the same level. We all begin our ascent from the valley: 'For all have sinned and fall short of the glory of God' (3:23). Remember, one of Paul's main aims in writing Romans was to establish unity between Jews and Gentiles. His unusual tactic seems to have been to offend everyone in equal measure! In Romans 1 Paul led *unrighteous sinners* down into *the valley of sin* by highlighting the sort of idolatry and sexual immorality characteristic of pagan Gentiles. However, all the while, Paul was laying a trap for religious types, which springs open in chapter 2.

Be careful when reading the Bible. Beneath the surface are hidden traps and it's easy to stumble into one without realising. In the New Testament, Jesus tells the story of the prodigal son with Pharisees (religious leaders) listening in. Imagine their smug smiles and judgmental thoughts as he described the rebellious son: *Yeah, you tell those filthy sinners!* But in the end, it's the self-righteous older brother who is left out in the cold. The parable was a trap, and the Pharisees knew it.

Now imagine Phoebe reading Romans chapter 1 to a house church gathered in Rome. As she described the downward slope of idolatry and sexual immorality, imagine Jewish Christians leaning in: *Yeah, sock it to those pork-eating, idol-worshipping, pansexual Gentiles!* The trap is set. Phoebe draws breath and launches into Romans chapter 2:

> If you think that leaves you on the high ground where you can point your finger at others, think again. Every time you criticize someone, you condemn yourself. It takes one to know one.
>
> *Romans 2:1 (MSG)*

If Romans 1 condemned *unrighteous* prodigal-types; Romans 2 turns on *self-righteous* Pharisee-types, who think their religious deeds put them in a different category. Paul probably has in mind Jewish believers who were tempted to assume that 'works of the Law' (especially circumcision, Sabbath and food laws) made them exempt from the wrath of God. This vital section (2:17—3:9) therefore highlights the failure of God's own people to keep the covenant he made with them.

> DIVINE SCRUTINY AT THE END WILL NOT SAY,
> 'TORAH PEOPLE TO MY RIGHT' AND 'NON-TORAH
> PEOPLE TO MY LEFT' . . . JUDGMENT WILL BE
> BASED NOT ON HISTORICAL PRIVILEGE BUT
> UPON CONFORMITY TO THE WILL OF GOD.
> Scot McKnight[13]

In Romans 2, Paul is therefore calling out a particular form of pride and hypocrisy that God's people have been guilty of since way back when. Though the specific issues may seem less relevant today, in truth many people still assume good works and religious commitments take them higher up the mountain. This kind of 'Moralism' may actually be the largest religion in the world. It does not have a box to tick on the census form, but so many Westerners assume that if there is a God, they would naturally be in credit. After all, compared to Hitler, Osama Bin Laden or people we've cancelled on social media, we are upstanding citizens who support charitable causes. Romans 2 pulls the rug from under proud feet and condemns this kind of Moralism as a false religion guilty of hypocrisy: 'you . . . pass judgment on them yet do the same things' (2:3).

As someone brought up in a Christian home and who has never been in trouble with the police, I regularly fall into this trap. Whenever I judge others, I fail to consider the shameful ways I have broken my own standards, let alone God's! And this despite the fact that I've had so many privileges and good influences. A Christian philosopher, Francis Schaeffer, once used a helpful illustration. Imagine every person has a voice recorder hung about their neck that captures the moral judgments with which they judge other people. Eventually, each person stands before God and he simply presses 'play' so each person hears in their own words all those statements by which they have assessed others. Then God simply says, 'Now where do you stand in the light of your own moral standards?'[14]

With this in mind, Paul poses a question that everyone must answer, whether religious-older-brother-types or rebellious-prodigal-son-types: 'Do you think you will escape God's judgment?' (2:3)

With Jew and Gentile equally offended, the atmosphere must have been awkward as Phoebe read on into chapter 3. In the concluding verses of this section, Paul takes both Jew and Gentile by the hand and brings them before the ultimate judge. Then, in the role of prosecutor, Paul gives his closing speech:

> Now we know that whatever the law says, it says to those who are under the law, so that every mouth may be silenced and the whole world held accountable to God.
>
> *Romans 3:19*

In a Roman court of law, when the defendant had nothing to say in their defence, they would put their hand over their mouth as a gesture of resignation. This is the place Romans 3 brings us to. If we are still wriggling with excuses, comparisons or counter-arguments, then perhaps we need to read through Romans 2 again. Ironically, only when we've looked up at the mountain from *the valley of sin* and concluded, 'I can't do this!' are we ready to begin the ascent. So if that's how you feel, take heart!

With all this in mind, let's wrap this chapter up with a couple of ways we can *look through* Romans and make sense of life.

Romans is a dose of *realism* that cultivates *honesty*

Western culture has been through a psychological revolution during the twentieth century, which has radically revised the way we think about ourselves. Helpful things have come from this, including a growing attentiveness to mental health and emotional wellbeing. However, what seems to have been lost in the process is a willingness to admit personal guilt or to consider the darker realities at work in you and me. Sophisticated people prefer to talk about obsessive behaviour, or neurotic patterns, or deviance, or pathology, or disorder. The language of sin has gradually faded out as a therapeutic culture aims to raise self-esteem. In order to improve the world and ourselves, we just need better education, greater social equality, more therapy and plenty of positive thinking.

However, despite what we've been *told about ourselves*, Romans resonates deeply with what we *know about ourselves*. There's something reassuring about owning the fact that we are flawed and guilty.[15] It feels honest. The alternative is that we over-compensate by trying harder, blaming society, playing the victim, judging others and showboating achievements. But this only fuels the sort of emotional insecurity and crushing expec-tation that causes anxiety and depression.

> THE LINE DIVIDING GOOD AND EVIL
> CUTS THROUGH THE HEART OF EVERY
> HUMAN BEING. AND WHO IS WILLING TO
> DESTROY A PIECE OF HIS OWN HEART?
> Aleksandr Solzhenitsyn in *The Gulag Archipelago*[16]

There's something refreshingly honest and strangely unifying about Romans 3:22–3: 'There is no difference . . . for all have sinned and fall short of the glory of God.' If each of us owned this reality, there would be a lot less pride, discrimination and hatred. Science, technology and education cannot fix our prob-lems. Romans is a dose of realism. We are not on an upward curve of enlightenment and progress, and the assumption that we are is a form of 'chronological snobbery'.[17] In ever more sophisticated ways we continue exactly the same pattern, exchanging 'the truth about God for a lie' and worshipping 'created things rather than the Creator' (1:25).

I believe this hard teaching is good for us, a pleasing pain that cultivates honesty. So much religion is superficial mask-wearing – putting on our Sunday best and pretending. Instead, if we embrace the truth that we are by nature broken, then what have we got to hide? We're sinners, aren't we? It's only pride that prevents us from being more open, honest and accountable with each other. What is the first step on the Alcoholics Anonymous programme? 'We admitted we were powerless over [our addiction] – that our lives had become unmanageable.'[18] An honest admission like this can be the first step toward freedom.

> ORIGINAL SIN IS THE MOST DEMOCRATIC
> OF THEOLOGICAL DOCTRINES – NONE
> OF US CAN ATTAIN PERFECTION, AND
> SO ALL OF US SHOULD SHOW HUMILITY
> IN OUR DEALINGS WITH OTHERS.
> Tom Holland, historian and author of *Dominion*[19]

Every Sunday in our church there is a moment of confession as we say together, 'Almighty God, our heavenly Father, we have sinned against you in thought and word and deed, through negligence, through weakness, through our own deliberate fault.' It's good for us because it's honest. God knows our kids need to say it! And they know that I need it too! Confession is an important part of being human. It opens the door to God and builds true friendship with others. The gospel tells us that all have sinned but all are welcome. Whether Arab or American, male or female, gay or straight. The toughest section of Romans is a dose of realism that cultivates honesty.

Romans is a dose of *optimism* that cultivates *hopefulness*

WHAT IS HAPPENING TO OUR YOUNG PEOPLE?
THEY DISOBEY THEIR PARENTS. THEY IGNORE
THE LAW. THEY RIOT IN THE STREETS. THEY
ARE INFLAMED WITH WILD PASSIONS.

Attributed to the philosopher Plato, fourth century BC

It's easy to assume the world is getting worse and the 'youth of today' are more sinful than ever. But Romans encourages a more optimistic view. Humans are no worse or better than they were in the first century. Despite the influence of mass media and social media, there is nothing fundamentally darker about the times we live in now.

Equally, the gospel is no less powerful than it was in the first century. If Paul can say in the face of the wickedness of Rome, 'I am not ashamed of the gospel' (1:16), then so can we! Romans does not encourage spiritual pessimism that gives up on the world, nor does it give us permission to moan about how terrible society has become. Instead, it can motivate a front-foot confidence in the gospel. The darker culture becomes, the brighter the gospel shines.

Having decided to ask Charlotte to marry me, I needed to get an engagement ring. So I went to the jewellers in Exeter where she lived and browsed some options in the cabinet. I then asked to view one that looked good. However, before the jeweller took out the ring, he spread out a black velvet cloth on the counter. Only then did he set down the ring, so that the diamond sparkled. Romans has laid out a dark backdrop. But now Paul is ready to bring out the diamond of the gospel so we can see it sparkle. Romans 1:18—3:20 is a dose of realism – we are all sinners in need of help. But it's also a dose of optimism. The gospel is still the good news that our sophisticated-but-sinful world desperately needs.

I got to know James while we were at university together. He was a smart dresser with a great sense of humour. On the surface, he had a lot going for him. When a mutual friend invited James to a Christian event we were hosting, he accepted. To my surprise, when we invited him along the next night, he accepted again. However, that proved to be a most uncomfortable evening! We sat through a blunt evangelistic message based on Romans 1—3. The former rugby player called Rico didn't pull any punches as he explained about sin and warned of judgment. He did go on to share the good news. But to me it felt too little, too late.

When the meeting finished, I stared straight ahead, not wanting to look at James. 'At least there's karaoke now,' I said, trying to lighten the mood.

Awkward silence.

'I'm really sorry if that offended you.'

Still no reply.

When I finally looked across at James, his eyes were full of tears. The tough message had hit home. After speaking further with Rico, that night James became an unlikely convert to Christianity. As he later admitted, he was unhappy with the way he was living. Deep down he knew it was wrong. Because Rico was honest enough to share the bad news, my friend came to believe the good news. James' story is a reminder that even the toughest sections of Romans still release the power of the gospel today.

REFLECT: Who do you most identify with: the *unrighteous* sinner in Romans 1 who rejects God's pattern, or the *self-righteous* person in Romans 2 who is prone to judging others?

Either way, the words of the Anglican liturgy help to confess our need of God:

Almighty God, our heavenly Father, we have sinned against you in thought and word and deed, through negligence, through weakness, through our own deliberate fault . . . We are truly sorry and repent of all our sins.

Anything specific? _____

There is no difference . . . for all have sinned and fall short of the glory of God.

Romans 3:22–3

3

The crux of salvation

Romans 3:21—4:25

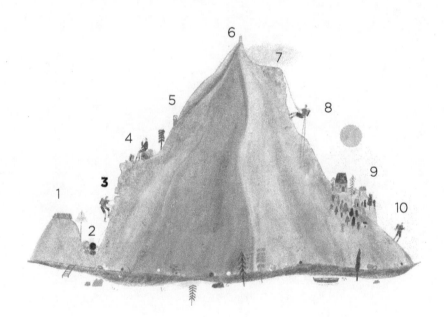

Every great story, whether an action-drama, a romantic comedy or a heroic tale, reaches a crisis moment. The protagonist appears done for. The music turns sinister, the shot closes in, all hope seems lost. Paul's letter to the Romans is no exception. Remember the key verse from our previous chapter: 'all have sinned and fall short of the glory of God' (3:23). Whether rebellious types (Gentiles) or religious types (Jews), there's no real difference. We have all exchanged the living God for idols and pointed the finger at others to mask our own failure.

The previous chapter left us all down in *the valley of sin*, facing the impenetrable cliff of God's justice. However, after the bad news, Paul is ready to reveal the good news. The narrative of Romans turns on two small words, like hinges that swing the whole letter in a new direction: 'But now . . .' (3:21). Paul often uses these words to introduce the crucial intervention of God precisely at the moment when all hope seems lost.[1] They indicate a switch of focus from the failure of humans to worship their creator to the faithfulness of God towards his creation.

This chapter is therefore entitled *The crux of salvation*. On a mountain climb, the crux pitch is the critical one. It's normally the hardest part of the route, involving the most technical climbing. But it's also the breakthrough moment. Get past the crux pitch, and the rest of the route opens up in an exhilarating way. That's Romans 3:21–31 – the most technical paragraph in the whole letter, but also the one that unlocks the route to the summit.

I also like the title of this chapter for another reason. Our word *crux* comes from the Latin word for *cross*. So when we say something is the crux of the matter, or 'crucial', we mean it is absolutely central, like the mid-point of a cross. As we will see, the crux of our salvation *is* the cross of Christ. The way out of our predicament in *the valley of sin* is not more effort on our part. Quite the opposite. It is to believe that Jesus' death has reconciled us to God. Having felt the crisis of sin, we're now ready to appreciate the beautiful diamond of grace.

Part 1: Justified by faith

We *look at* Romans 3:21–6 to understand what God has done to save us through the death of Christ. This paragraph is quite technical. So get ready for another challenge!

○─○ Part 2: Living by faith

We will *look through* Romans chapter 4 and consider the example of Abraham. He inspires us not only to be justified by faith but also to live a life of adventure.

> [We] are justified freely by his grace through the redemption that came by Christ Jesus.
>
> *Romans 3:24*

Part 1: Justified by faith

READ: Romans 3:21–31

At the beginning of the letter, Paul declared that the gospel reveals 'the righteousness of God' (1:17). Now Paul is ready to explain why this is such good news. At the heart of the Christian message is a profound question: How can a just and holy God declare sinners to be righteous? This conundrum is so significant that Romans 3:21–6 has been described as 'the chief and very central place of the whole Bible' and 'the most important paragraph ever written'.[2]

However, in our cultural context we may be forgiven for wondering, 'Is it still relevant?' Most of my friends seem less bothered about how to be put right with God and more concerned about which channel has the rights for the sport they want to watch. Until the second half of the twentieth century, Western culture largely believed in the notion of personal guilt and divine judgment. That's why the simple message of the American evangelist, Billy Graham, proved so effective. However, over recent decades we have witnessed a major shift in cultural sensibilities.

So has Paul's paragraph lost its appeal? Is the Bible answering questions we're no longer asking? Perhaps. But it's important to remember that just because certain truths go out of fashion, that doesn't make them irrelevant. As many cancer patients will tell you, it's possible to live with a serious underlying condition but to be blissfully unaware of it – at least for a while. Let me illustrate on a lighter note. A few months ago, I was on a conference call when the doorbell rang. It was a pest-control company called 'Mouse Arrest'! I was so annoyed by this interruption that I practically slammed the door in their face. They responded by pushing a business card through the letter box to spite me.

A few months later, while lying in bed, I heard them . . . scratch . . . scratch . . . eek . . . eek. My response was, 'Where did I put that business card?!' A rude interruption was now vital information.

So it is with the gospel. What may seem like an interruption proves to be a source of good news once we appreciate the serious predicament we are in. Sin is not a little pest that goes away with a quick fix. It is an infestation of the heart. What I am highlighting is that our culture's initial response to the gospel may be hostile or indifferent. Nevertheless, in quiet moments, when guilt and shame scratch away at our conscience, the letter of Romans is just the place we need to turn.

With this in mind, the key verse for this chapter builds on last time. Put them together and they sum up Paul's argument in the first section of Romans:

> There is no difference between Jew and Gentile, for all have sinned and fall short of the glory of God, and all are justified freely by his grace.
>
> *Romans 3:22–4*

To be justified or declared righteous means to be absolved of guilt and therefore accepted and approved of. Think of it like a performance review or a CV that you submit as part of an application. If your record is considered good enough, it opens doors and secures you a place. Many people assume Christianity is about building up sufficient moral credit to impress God and secure a place in heaven. That's why Christians think they're better than others, right? Wrong. That's the exact opposite of Paul's argument. The arresting phrase, 'But now' (3:21), introduces a new idea that other religions simply can't accommodate. According to the gospel, righteousness or 'justification' is an unmerited gift, not a hard-earned wage.

During a British conference on comparative religions, experts from around the world debated what, if any, belief was unique to the Christian faith. The debate went on for some time until C. S. Lewis wandered into the room. 'What's the rumpus about?' he asked, and heard in reply that his colleagues were discussing Christianity's unique contribution among world religions. Lewis responded, 'Oh, that's easy. It's grace!'[3]

The notion of God's love as a free gift sets Christianity apart from the Buddhist eightfold path, the Hindu doctrine of karma, the Jewish Torah and the Muslim code of law. They offer a way to earn approval. Only Christianity dares to offer salvation entirely as a gift. This is very good news for those who feel morally bankrupt. It also silences boasting and bragging rights. Romans is the reversal of self-righteous, DIY religion. Instead, *the crux of salvation* is the cross of Christ. In Romans 3:21–6, Paul draws on three metaphors to explain how this works:

Slave market redemption

All are justified freely by his grace through the *redemption* that came by Christ Jesus.

Romans 3:24 (italics added)

'Redemption' refers to the emancipation of a slave through payment of what was known as the ransom price. Remember, at least one-third of the population of Rome would have been slaves in the first century AD. Many were captured in foreign lands and brought to Rome as human machines. Once in the city, they would have been sold in slave markets to merchants needing cheap labour. Imagine men, women and children being paraded past shoppers with price tags around their necks. Apparently, if they wore a cap in the market it meant a no-returns policy. They really were treated like machines.

Now imagine Phoebe reading this section of Romans to Gentile Christians meeting secretly in a poor part of the city. How might these words have sounded to a slave who knew what it felt like to be sold in the market? In Jesus Christ, God has stepped in to pay our ransom or freedom price. When we were trapped like a slave in the market, Jesus died to liberate us.

Equally, Jewish Christians would have connected the idea of redemption to the Exodus story. When the people of Israel were enslaved under the boot of Pharaoh, God brought a series of plagues, culminating in the death of the firstborn and the Passover event – a spotless lamb was sacrificed and blood daubed on doorposts to save Israel from the angel of death. As a result, God's people were set free. The ransom price was the Passover Lamb. That's why Paul declares that redemption is 'through the shedding of [Christ's] blood' (3:25). He is our Passover Lamb. By his blood, we have been redeemed. Whether slaves or masters, Jews or Gentiles, the message is clear: Jesus has paid our ransom price. When we turned our back on God, he purchased our freedom.

One of my favourite musicals, *Les Misérables*, has a poignant scene which captures the essence of redemption. The shady character, Jean Valjean, has taken refuge in a monastery, where a kind bishop has given him dinner and a bed for the night. However, despite his generosity, the bishop catches him stealing the silverware. Valjean strikes the bishop in the face and runs away into the night.

The next day, Valjean is caught by the gendarmes and returned to the monastery. In a deeply moving scene, the bishop insists that he gave the silverware to Valjean and asks him in front of the policemen, 'Why didn't you take the silver candlesticks as well? They are worth 2,000 francs!' The bishop is determined to give Valjean a new start at his own expense.

Later on, in a private conversation, Valjean asks the bishop, 'Why are you doing this?' to which he replies, 'Jean Valjean, my brother, you no longer belong to evil. With this silver, I've bought your soul. I've *ransomed* you from fear and hatred. And now I give you back to God!'[4]

Redemption pays the price in order to buy us back from evil. However miserably we have failed in the past, Jesus sets us free to live a new life. As we'll see in Romans 6—7, this is more than just forgiveness. Redemption also includes being set free from the reign of sin so we can live with dignity and purpose.

Temple sacrifice

God presented Christ as a *sacrifice* of atonement, through the shedding of his blood.

Romans 3:25

Offering sacrifices was like paying taxes in the Roman world. On a regular basis, you would present an animal or liquid offering (libation) to a relevant god in exchange for protection and peace. In this context, imagine how bizarre it would have sounded that God had offered the sacrifice for you! This complete role reversal gives an indication of how radical the gospel is. Instead of you paying the gods, God pays for you.

Today, we may not visit temples. But we all make sacrifices for modern gods we serve. When we make money our idol, we work ourselves into the ground trying to feel secure. When we make pleasure our idol, we chase experiences and relationships in a restless quest to be satisfied. Twenty-first-century gods still demand sacrifice. To those feeling exhausted by this continual need to impress, accumulate and achieve, the gospel is such good news. There's nothing we need to do to buy God's favour. He offered the perfect sacrifice himself.

The Jewish temple context makes sense of Paul's careful phrase: 'a sacrifice of atonement [*hilastērion*]' (3:25). Deep in the heart of the temple was the 'most holy place' or 'Holy of holies'. Thought to be God's throne room, this space housed the Ark of the Covenant – a large rectangular box which contained the stone tablets with the Ten Commandments written on them. This was covered by a lid known as the 'mercy seat' (Greek *hilastērion*), which is the very term Paul used in Romans 3:25 as he drew on the Greek translation of the Hebrew

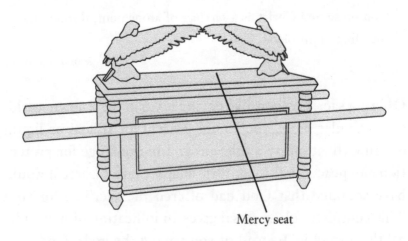

Mercy seat

Scriptures known as the Septuagint. The mercy seat was adorned with solid gold cherubim at either end (Exod. 25:17–22). When sacrifices were made on the annual Day of Atonement (*Yom Kippur*), blood from the offering was brought into the holy of holies and sprinkled over the mercy seat by the High Priest (see Leviticus 16:13–15). The symbolism was clear – only the blood of a perfect sacrifice could atone for or cover over the law-breaking guilt of God's people.

Paul deliberately compares the sacrifice of Christ with this Old Testament tradition. As the blood of an animal symbolised atonement for Israel, so the sacrifice of Jesus purifies us from all sin. Christ's blood shed on the cross is therefore the most powerful cleansing agent. As the old hymn puts it:

What can wash away my sin?
Nothing but the blood of Jesus.
What can make me whole again?
Nothing but the blood of Jesus.

Robert Lowry (1826–1899)

The detail about the mercy seat may sound rather complicated. But don't be put off. The good news is, we don't need to understand justification by faith to be justified by faith! We simply need to believe in the work of Jesus Christ and the gift of righteousness becomes ours. That's why Paul can argue that justification works backwards, through the Old Testament, as well as forward to us (3:25). Even Abraham, who lived *c.*1800 BC and didn't know the name 'Jesus', was justified by trusting the promise of God to provide salvation. So our faith does not depend on understanding complex theory but on trusting in a person, Jesus Christ: 'This is why the fulfilment of God's promise depends entirely on trusting God and his way ... God's promise arrives as pure gift' (Rom. 4:16, MSG).

Law Court justice

[God] did it to demonstrate his righteousness at the present time, so as to be *just* and the one who *justifies* those who have faith in Jesus.

Romans 3:26

Paul now draws on a legal metaphor to help us understand justification. His argument revolves around a versatile Greek stem (*dikai*), which lies at the heart of words we translate as 'justice', 'righteousness', 'justified'. Through a play on words, Paul is therefore able to show that God's *justice* and our *justification* are two sides of the same coin. In verse 25 Paul has already noted that God 'left the sins committed beforehand unpunished'. Throughout the Old Testament, animal sacrifices were only a signpost, pointing towards a future moment when God's justice would need to be properly satisfied. This came to a head around April AD 30, when Jesus the Messiah was crucified on a Roman cross. As the perfect human, Jesus offered his life on behalf of sinful humans. On the cross, God's standards of justice were therefore satisfied *and* our sin was atoned for.

BOTH GOD'S LOVE AND GOD'S WRATH ARE RATCHETED UP IN THE MOVE FROM THE OLD TESTAMENT TO THE NEW ... THESE THEMES BARREL ALONG THROUGH REDEMPTIVE HISTORY, UNRESOLVED, UNTIL THEY COME TO A RESOUNDING CLIMAX IN THE CROSS.

D. A. Carson[5]

According to Paul's metaphor in Romans 3, through the cross of Christ we are legally justified before God. The case against us, which we considered in the previous chapter, is formally closed. Imagine a defendant in a court of law, who knows they are guilty as charged. And yet, through the intervention of a friend, the verdict swings the other way. They are acquitted and declared 'not guilty'. Imagine the feeling going through them as the judge's gavel hammers down and closes the case! This is the outcome every time someone believes in Jesus. The case against us is dropped and we are declared righteous. As Paul puts it in one of his other letters: 'God . . . forgave us all our sins, having cancelled the charge of our legal indebtedness, which stood against us and condemned us; he has taken it away, nailing it to the cross' (Col. 2:13–14).

In verse 26, Paul therefore loops back to the idea he introduced in chapter 1, but now gives it fuller meaning: the 'righteousness of God' (1:17) is revealed through the event of the cross which satisfied the judicial penalty related to our sin: 'he did it to demonstrate his righteousness . . . so as to be just and the one who justifies those who have faith in Jesus' (3:26).

A child-friendly definition of justification expresses it this way: just as if I'd never sinned. God no longer sees our guilt or failure. Instead, we are righteous in his sight and welcomed into his covenant people, regardless of our ethnicity or morality. This is justification. It includes both a vertical dimension – we are put right with God – and a horizontal dimension – we become part of God's family and enjoy fellowship around the table together.

So the smallest phrase in Romans 3:21, 'But now', is an important milestone in our ascent of Romans. Having been led down into *the valley of sin*, now the route turns in a different direction. The cross of Christ lifts us up through *the crux of salvation*. By grace, we find ourselves on the right side of God's justice. The 'righteousness of God' has dealt with the 'wrath of God' (1:17, 18) in a way that fully satisfied the justice of God (3:26). Two small words have made all the difference.

During a severe potato famine in Ireland, several families wrote letters to their landlord saying they had absolutely no money to pay their rent and begged to be let off their debts. The Irish landlord, Canon Andrew Robert Fausset, wrote back to his tenants and explained that it was quite impossible to let them off their debts. It would set a bad precedent. They had to pay every single penny. '*But*,' he wrote, 'I enclose something that might help.'[6] He sent a cheque for a very large sum of money, which more than covered all their debts. Their hearts must have leapt with joy as they read that word '*But*'. In the same way, Romans 3:21 indicates a complete reversal of fortunes. Through faith in Jesus, the crucified Messiah, our debts are paid and we are forgiven and set free.

REFLECT: Watch the scene in *Les Misérables* with Jean Valjean and the priest, or listen to the famous hymn 'Amazing Grace'. Can you pick out the themes of justice, atonement and justification?

○─○ Part 2: Living by faith

READ: Romans 4:1–25

On our adventure through Romans, we've made it past the crux pitch (Rom. 3:21–6). From here the terrain gets easier. Soon we will stop for a rest and reflect on the ground covered so far (Rom. 5). First, however, we must follow some ancient footprints through the next section. Having *looked at* Romans to see what it means to be justified by faith, we now *look through* Romans to see what it means to live by faith.

In Romans 4, Paul turns to the Old Testament character of Abraham – the patriarch or founding father of Israel. Remember, God's *call* to Abraham in Genesis 12 was a direct response to the *fall* of humanity in Genesis 3. Through his family, all that had gone wrong with the world would be reversed. The curses would become blessings once more as Abraham's offspring became a single worldwide family (Gen. 12:3). Indeed, God's faithful action to fulfil his promises to Abraham would in time restore hope to the whole world, including the natural environment.

When I read through Romans on my Kindle, with the Milky Way shimmering overhead, I was struck by the scale of Paul's vision in Romans 4. He clearly has Psalm 2 in mind, in which the Messiah inherits Abraham's blessing in such a way that the nations become his inheritance and the ends of the earth his possession. That's why Paul can say that 'Abraham and his offspring received the promise that he would be *heir of the world*' (4:13, italics added). What a breathtaking vision!

With this in mind, Abraham is not just a character study but the archetypal figure for the people of God. Abraham defines, more than anyone else, who is truly 'justified' and part of the people of God. In Genesis 12, God called Abraham while he was still an idol-worshipping pagan. Despite being seventy-five years old and childless, God made extraordinary promises to him and his wife Sarah. Their descendants would become more numerous than the sand on the shore or the stars in the sky. By the way, scientists estimate that there are actually more stars than grains of sand in the universe. Imagine that! To inherit these incredible promises, Abraham and Sarah had to believe God and step out in faith – literally. They relocated to the land of Canaan (the Promised Land) and the nation of Israel was born.

In Romans 4, Paul unpacks Abraham's story because it reveals God's original pattern of salvation. Far from Abraham working his way to God through impressive moral endeavour, God came to Abraham while he was lost in *the valley of sin* and called him into a new life. To receive this new identity, blessing and purpose, Abraham simply had to believe. One memorable night, God called him out of the confines of his nomadic tent and made an extraordinary promise. By the way, this turns out to be the most quoted Old Testament passage in the New Testament:

[God] said, 'Look up at the sky and count the stars – if indeed you can count them.' Then he said to him, 'So shall your offspring be.'

Abram believed the LORD, and he credited it to him as righteousness.

Genesis 15:5–6

At this point in his life, Abraham was not yet circumcised, nor did he have the Torah. Moses came much later. But simply by believing God's promise of good news, Abraham was declared to be righteous. So salvation by faith goes all the way back! For Jew and Gentile, circumcised and uncircumcised, it's always been the only way to be put right with God and to become part of his covenant people.

> THE RESULT IS THAT ALL THOSE WHO BELIEVE IN 'THE GOD WHO RAISED JESUS FROM THE DEAD' CONSTITUTE THE SINGLE FAMILY PROMISED BY COVENANT TO ABRAHAM. ABRAHAM'S OWN FAITH . . . DESPITE HIS AND SARAH'S OLD AGE, BECOMES THE PARADIGM FOR THE FAITH BY WHICH THE SIN-FORGIVEN FAMILY IS NOW MARKED OUT.
>
> N. T. Wright and M. F. Bird[7]

Salvation then is not a tick-box exercise. It is a gift of grace that calls us into an adventure of faith. Now, Paul invites us to 'follow in the footsteps of . . . our father Abraham' (Rom. 4:12). What a great metaphor for our ascent of Romans! After a steep climb through Romans 1—3, it's as if we clamber over the horizon only to discover a set of footprints. Long before we got here, Father Abraham was justified by faith. Now we are invited to follow his tracks. Here are a couple of specific ways to do this:

How to follow Abraham's footsteps?
Be grateful not boastful (4:1–5)

If, in fact, Abraham was justified by works, he had something to boast about – but not before God. What does Scripture say?

'Abraham believed God, and it was credited to him as righteousness.'

Now to the one who works, wages are not credited as a gift but as an obligation. However, to the one who does not work but trusts God who justifies the ungodly, their faith is credited as righteousness.

Romans 4:2–5

The first thing Paul highlights is that justification is a gift, not a wage. A valuable status has been credited to our account ('right-eousness'), but somebody else paid for it. If you were to receive an expensive gift for your birthday, it would be totally inappropriate to boast of how much you can afford. Instead, you would be so grateful to the one who bought you the gift. If our good works justified us, then we might have something to brag about, 'but not before God' (4:2). The only thing we have contributed to our salvation is sin. Otherwise, Christ has footed the entire bill. The judge took our judgment so that we might enjoy his grace.

When we experience this personally, it stirs a deep sense of gratitude. We come to view all of life as a gift, not a right. Abraham did not earn the Promised Land but worshipped God for the gift. It doesn't matter how many years I've been preach-ing sermons or going on mission, my service to God is not a mortgage repayment. Salvation is a gift. The only response God is looking for is joyful thanks and generous living that expresses our deep reliance on him.

However, this sort of vision is countercultural. Through media channels and advertising, we are encouraged to insist on our rights and push for what we're entitled to. We want to be self-made, autonomous people who can be proud of what we've achieved. The idea of receiving charity insults our pride.

Another dramatic scene in *Les Misérables* captures the moment when Inspector Javert is forced to accept that he owes his life to the common criminal, Jean Valjean. Rather than show gratitude for his act of mercy, Javert commits suicide. Because he only knows law, merit, and reward, he cannot live with his need of grace. There is a Javert in all of us. If we won't accept our need of grace, our hearts will become hardened by pride and bitterness or our souls will sink into resentment and spiritual depression. The footsteps of Father Abraham take us in a different direction.

As a young pastor, I went to visit an older member of the congregation, called Hedley, who was housebound. Hedley had recently undergone surgery but, owing to a medical error, he was now in considerable pain and unlikely to make a full recovery. When I asked Hedley the polite question, 'How are you?' his response caught my attention.

'I have much to thank the Lord for!' he said with a warm smile. There was sincerity behind this statement. It felt like it came from a deep place, given the circumstances he was in.

From then on, I visited Hedley once a week – mainly because I needed more of what he had! Each time we read a chapter of Romans and prayed together.

Just before we reached the end of Paul's letter, Hedley died. I felt such a loss, even though we were only just getting to know each other. His disposition of gratitude, his refusal to entertain bitterness or blame others – these were the marks of grace, and they left a deep impression on me.

According to the first three chapters of Romans, if we want to talk about what we *deserve* or what we are *entitled* to, then Paul would say, 'Good luck!' Are you sure you want to appeal to the righteous judge, who knows every secret, on that basis?' Instead, Abraham's example leads us into a life of unceasing gratitude and deep reliance on God. Whatever happens, whether I get a pay rise or face redundancy; whether the test results are benign or malignant; whether I fall in love or feel alone – I am a recipient of amazing grace. As Hedley would put it, 'I have much to thank the Lord for!' Gratitude is the way to start and end the day and the basis for how we treat others.[8] In the end, I am not a Christian because I am a better person. It is all a gift.

How to follow Abraham's footsteps?
Be adventurous not cautious (4:18–25)

> Without weakening in his faith, [Abraham] faced the fact that his body was as good as dead – since he was about a hundred years old – and that Sarah's womb was also dead. Yet he did not waver through unbelief regarding the promise of God, but was strengthened in his faith and gave glory to God, being fully persuaded that God had power to do what he had promised.
>
> *Romans 4:19–21*

Justification is not simply a doctrine in a creed to give assent to. It also involves putting truth into practice and stepping out in faith. The footsteps of Abraham and Sarah led on into a life of adventure. In this sense, faith is a two-sided coin. It is both a gift from God that enables us to receive salvation (saved by faith) and also an active trust that steps into the promises of God (living by faith). In the case of Abraham and Sarah, living by faith involved travelling nine hundred miles from their homeland and living a nomadic existence in Canaan or the Promised Land. There they faced numerous threats and at times gave into fear and took matters into their own hands.

So take heart if you feel weak and fragile. At times, the odds will appear to be stacked against the promises of God. But nevertheless, Abraham and Sarah moved halfway across the Middle East based on a promise and without any deposit. Now that's faith. It's the adventure of trusting God in spite of what we see around us: Abraham 'faced the fact that his body was as good as dead' (v. 19). Like Abraham, we may feel challenged by the realities we see in front of us. Yet our ultimate confidence rests in the power of God.

Even after God miraculously provided a son for Abraham and Sarah in their old age, they still had to trust through testing times. The adventure of faith never ends. On one occasion, God called Abraham to go up a mountain, Mount Moriah, and there to sacrifice the promised child, Isaac (Gen. 22). Once again, Abraham stepped out in faith and trusted God despite not having a clue how things would turn out. In the end, God himself provided a ram as a sacrifice instead of Isaac.

This story may seem strange, even offensive, to our ears. But don't miss the big idea. High on Mount Moriah, Abraham took a step of faith and God himself provided the sacrifice. Centuries later, on a rocky outcrop called Golgotha on the edge of Mount Moriah, Jesus made the ultimate sacrifice for us on the cross. Our Father in heaven would sooner give up his own son than break a promise he has made. So, like Abraham, whatever God asks of us, we can trust he has a good outcome in mind.

AS ABRAHAM CONTEMPLATED HIS AGE
AND SARAH'S BARRENNESS, HE NEITHER
TURNED A BLIND EYE TO THESE PROBLEMS
NOR UNDERESTIMATED THEM. BUT HE
REMINDED HIMSELF OF GOD'S POWER AND
FAITHFULNESS. FAITH ALWAYS LOOKS AT THE
PROBLEMS IN THE LIGHT OF THE PROMISES.

John Stott[9]

I wonder what it means for you to see your *problems* in the light of God's *promises*. When we face setbacks and disappointments, it's easy to become risk-averse and settle for a cautious life. Christians can end up living like *practical atheists*. Though we believe in God, we keep everything under our control. However, the more we meditate on God's amazing grace, the more we are liberated from small-minded, fearful living. Having been justified by grace, we can step out in faith. After all, it's not the size of our faith but the faithfulness of God that matters. Abraham believed and God never let him down, even when Abraham made foolish or fearful decisions (Gen. 12:10–20; 20:1–18). In the same way, justification by faith secures us to God and gives us confidence to step out in faith.

On a recent climbing trip with my son, we reached a rather steep and exposed section. So I tied a rope around his waist and went on ahead of him. Once I was anchored to the rock, he followed and I took in the rope. He had freedom to go for it because he was roped to me. He may have slipped, but as his father I would not let him fall. In the same way, justification by faith ties us into a covenant relationship with God. Secure in the knowledge that our heavenly Father has got us, we can follow in the adventurous footsteps of Abraham and Sarah.

I wonder what God is calling you to do? Perhaps to get baptised if you haven't already? Or take on a new ministry responsibility? Or pioneer a social project? Or share your faith with colleagues? Or invite someone else to journey through Romans with you? God's grace frees us to go for it. We have been ransomed from sin and justified for ever. What have we got to lose? As Paul says later in Romans, 'If God is for us, who can be against us?' (8:31). Nothing 'will be able to separate us from the love of God' (8:39).

A few years ago, we stayed in a beautiful apartment in a ski resort in France. My wife's relative owned the accommodation and also a posh restaurant beneath it. They insisted that we dine there during our stay, and I was keen on the idea . . . until I saw the menu. Evening dinner was a standard seven-course meal with almost as many noughts on the price. The food turned out to be delicious, but throughout the dinner I was cautious, trying to limit the damage. 'Let's just have tap water; no need for wine!'

At the end of the meal, I got out my wallet and went to pay.

'No, sir!' the waiter insisted. 'The owner has paid the bill!'

I can't describe the relief I felt . . . along with some regret. I wanted to order from the menu all over again: 'Let's have steak and wine!'

The waiter's announcement captures the heart of the gospel that we have unpacked in this section of Romans: 'The owner has paid the bill!' Our creator has redeemed us with his own blood. We are justified freely by his grace. Now a life of adventure awaits us. So let's not play it safe and be left with regret. Through faith in the Messiah, we become part of a magnificent drama that stretches back to Abraham. Now we are on the other side of Pentecost, empowered by the Holy Spirit to live bold and generous lives. Faith makes us part of this great story, which is all underwritten by the faithfulness of God.

REFLECT

Like Abraham, we all face challenges and disappointments. What are some of yours? But what promises has God given to you and your family from Scripture? Identify a key verse or phrase and stick it somewhere memorable (for example, make it your screen saver or stick it to your fridge door).

[We] are justified freely by his grace through the redemption that came by Christ Jesus.

Romans 3:24

4

The place of peace

Romans 5:1–21

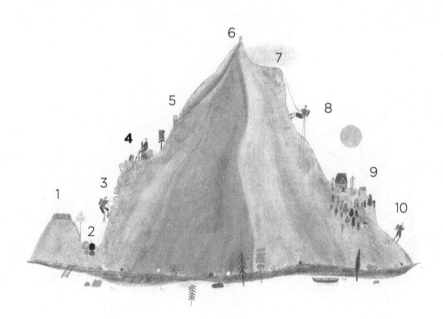

Romans 5 begins with 'Therefore' (5:1). When we read this word in Paul's letters, it's good to ask, 'What is it *there for?*' Invariably, Paul uses 'therefore' to indicate a change of pace and a chance to reflect on things. This is the purpose of Romans 5. It's a place to rest, an opportunity to pause and take in the personal implications of the teaching we have covered so far. Here, weary souls can recover.

I love these moments on big mountain days. You've sweated your way up steep terrain, faced some challenging sections. Then you come over a horizon onto easier ground. Now it's time to sit down, take a breather and get the flask and sandwiches out. As your head lifts, you begin to appreciate the scale of the view that has been developing behind you. You're higher than you thought you were. Now you can see why the route so far made sense – we had to descend into *the valley of sin* (1:18—3:20), face *the crux of salvation* (3:21–31) and follow the footsteps of Abraham (4:1–25) in order to get to this amazing vantage point. From here we can also see the narrow ridge that lies ahead and glimpse the summit peak for the first time.

Well done! You've made it to Romans 5 – *the place of peace*.

In this chapter, we will reflect on what the gospel means for us at a more personal level and bask in the extraordinary view of God's love.

 ## Part 1: God's peace is a certain fact

We will consider how God has demonstrated his love through the death of Christ and by giving us a new status (justification) and a new standing in grace.

 ## Part 2: God's peace is a lived experience

We will consider how the Holy Spirit helps us experience God's love personally and how this changes the way we see all of life, including hard times of suffering.

> God demonstrates his own love for us in this: while we were still sinners, Christ died for us.
>
> *Romans 5:8*

Part 1: God's peace is a certain fact

READ: Romans 5:1–11

If you'd ever met my wife, Charlotte, you'd know she's too good for me. But despite my many faults and failings, including throwing my wedding ring away in front of her (you will have to read my first book to put that in context), twenty years on we're still happily married.

Now, imagine someone should ask, 'But how do you know you are married? How can you be sure?' I might respond in a couple of ways. I could provide legal evidence that proves it. My marriage certificate, for example. It bears witness to a particular moment when we entered a covenant relationship with binding vows before many witnesses. So there are objective facts. But if that was the only proof, you might be worried! We also communicate our love to each other in various ways on a daily basis. In other words, *subjective* experiences flow out of the *objective* fact. Both bear witness to a deep and profound reality.

Like a marriage, our relationship with God is built on objective facts and lived experiences. In Romans 5, Paul shares profound reasons to be confident that God loves us. There is a legal basis to our relationship: a binding covenant has been signed in blood. The Holy Spirit also communicates this love to us in more subjective ways that put the heart and soul into Christianity. The underlying goal as we consider Romans 5, particularly focusing on verses 1–11, is that our spiritual assurance and confidence increase.

Do you sometimes doubt God's love? It's common to feel a sense of failure and self-condemnation that leaves us questioning how God feels about us. I may be more convinced that God loves *you* but struggle to believe that he loves *me*. How would you rate your assurance of God's love right now?

1	2	3	4	5
PLAGUED BY DOUBT	VERY UNCERTAIN	UP & DOWN	MOSTLY CONFIDENT	FULLY ASSURED

My prayer is that through this chapter we will move further to the right and remain there even in the tough times of life.

Paul's opening phrase conveys the basis of our assurance: 'Therefore, since we have been justified through faith, we have peace with God' (5:1). The shock here is the certainty with which Paul speaks about our status before God. Notice he uses the past tense. We've already been justified. To religious ears, the language of justification is an end-time verdict that belongs in the future. Life is like a moral exam. Only at the end will we find out whether we passed, right? Wrong. Paul deliberately declares in the past tense a verdict that other religions leave hanging in the future. You can know *now* that you are eternally loved and accepted by God.

How is this possible? Well, Romans 1—4 made clear it is not based on our own merit. Paul was careful to condemn both Jew and Gentile, religious and irreligious, before the divine judge. Remember, 'all have sinned and fall short of the glory of God' (3:23)? So our confidence must not be rooted in ourselves. As Abraham revealed, justification is not a wage but a gift: we are 'justified freely by his grace' (3:24). Christ took our guilt to the cross so that we could be declared righteous simply by faith. Most people understand religion as some form of moral pilgrimage, with the final outcome uncertain. But the unique thing about the gospel is that it gives the result upfront.

To illustrate how this works, I often tell the story of what happened when I completed my PhD several years ago. In the British system, this involves writing an 80,000-word thesis which is then submitted to academic experts for review. A few weeks later, you attend a *viva voce* examination to defend your work. The academics grill you for several hours before conferring to reach a decision. They then call you back in to tell you whether you've passed or not. Years of hard work come down to one nerve-racking meeting. However, in my case, something unusual happened. After exchanging initial pleasantries, the lead examiner announced, 'We've decided to tell you in advance that you've passed. Well done, Dr Ollerton!' With that, he thrust out his hand and we shook on it. Before answering a single question, I was 'Dr Ollerton'. As their decision sank in, I experienced a deep sense of peace. Over the next couple of hours, we went on to discuss the ways I could improve my work. Only, now I could embrace their feedback, secure in the knowledge that I had passed.

This is the kind of assurance that justification brings. Through faith in Christ, God declares his acceptance of us upfront and confers a new status on us. We are righteous in God's sight and deeply loved by him. Of course, there is still much to improve. But we start the Christian life secure in the love of God.

In this chapter, we are primarily focusing on Romans 5:1–11. However, the second half of Romans chapter 5 (vv. 12–21) goes on to explain how God could declare us 'righteous' even though we were sinners. To do this, Paul draws on a comparison between two representative figures: Adam, the first man, and Christ, the new Adam. The technical term is that they are 'federal heads'. Imagine two football teams lining up in the tunnel before running out onto the pitch. Twenty-one players line up behind two captains who stand at the head of their team. In the same way, Paul considers the entire human race to be aligned with one of two representatives. We are either 'in Adam' or 'in Christ'. Notice the difference is not whether we are Jew or Gentile – ethnicity is irrelevant – or whether we are 'good' or 'bad' – morality is irrelevant. It's whether we line up behind Christ by faith or whether we remain part of the old, fallen human race as represented by Adam.

> THERE ARE TWO WAYS: ONE THAT BEGINS
> WITH ADAM AND ONE THAT BEGINS WITH
> CHRIST. ADAM IS A TRAGEDY; CHRIST
> IS REDEMPTION FROM TRAGEDY.
> Scot McKnight[1]

All the way back in Genesis 3, sin and death entered the world as a result of Adam and Eve's rebellion against God. Ever since, humans have been born into this predicament so that, like Adam and Eve, we succumb to a life of sin and death. However, just as the first man brought the whole human race down, so Christ has begun a new humanity characterised by righteousness and life. Here's how Paul puts it:

> The judgment followed one sin and brought condemnation, but the gift followed many trespasses and brought justification.
>
> *Romans 5:16*

Consequently, just as one trespass resulted in condemnation for all people, so also one righteous act resulted in justification and life for all people.

Romans 5:18

By nature, we are born into a fallen human race. But by grace we can be born again into a new humanity that lines up behind Christ. Salvation is far more radical than merely believing some truths and living a better life. It's being transferred from one team to another. This spiritual relocation brings with it a new identity and a new set of privileges. I often illustrate this by taking a miniature card person and placing them inside a book, like a bookmark. Imagine this book is entitled 'Adam'. If the cardboard person is placed inside this book, they will be judged by that front cover. However, what if we then take the figure out of that book and transfer them into another book entitled 'Jesus'. Now they are 'in Christ'. So they will be judged by his status. This is what it means to be justified. Regardless of who we are or what we've done, we are transferred into Jesus Christ. We belong to him through a new covenant agreement written in his blood. We are 'in Christ' and therefore God's love for us is as certain as his love for Jesus!

In verse 2, Paul goes on to describe the difference this makes, the benefits that flow from being 'in Christ'. He outlines two realities that belong to Jesus but have now become ours.

Peace with God

THEREFORE, SINCE WE HAVE BEEN JUSTIFIED
THROUGH FAITH, WE HAVE *peace with God*
THROUGH OUR LORD JESUS CHRIST.

Romans 5:1 (italics added)

In our frantic world, the idea of peace is appealing – a warm feeling of tranquillity. But to have this experience of peace, we first need to know that there is foundational peace. As with a marriage, the subjective experience flows from the objective fact. So the focus of Romans 5 is less on the peace *of* God – for that see Philippians 4:7 – and more about peace *with* God. If we want to enjoy a life of inner peace, we first need to know that God's wrath has ended and we are right with our maker.

In verses 9–10, Paul gives the basis for such confidence:

> Since we have now been justified by his blood, how much more shall we be saved from God's wrath through him! For if, while we were God's enemies, we were reconciled to him through the death of his Son, how much more, having been reconciled, shall we be saved through his life!

One of my favourite places to visit in Rome is a beautifully preserved stone structure known as *Ara Pacis* or 'the altar of peace'. It was built in the first century to commemorate the reign of Caesar Augustus who brought victory, wealth and expansion to Rome. By the way, did you know that the month of 'August' was named after him – and July after 'Julius' Caesar? Anyway, the reign of Augustus secured what was known as *pax Romana*, or Roman peace. However, this kind of peace was achieved through putting enemies to the sword. It was their blood on the altar. In Romans 5, Paul deliberately contrasts the way of the Caesars with Christ. Instead of peace being achieved by the blood of his enemies, God has made peace through the blood of his Son shed on the cross. Jesus is the true peacemaker for all humanity – Romans and barbarians, Black and White, rich and poor. Jesus' blood established a permanent peace treaty between God and us.

Imagine it like the Christmas truce of 1914. During the First World War, British and German troops were at war. On 23 December they were shelling each other in brutal trench warfare. But on 24 December a Christmas ceasefire was declared. Troops emerged from their dugouts and met in no-man's-land. They shared stories and cigarettes, sang carols and played football. Apparently, the Germans won on penalties! Once peace was declared, hostilities ceased and the soldiers were able to enjoy a new experience. It was not based on a feeling or improved behaviour but on a formal treaty.

Sadly, by Boxing Day, the conflict had resumed.

It's easy for us to imagine that peace with God is also fragile. If we sin or slip up, the fun is over and God turns against us. But if we are 'in Christ', God's love is a permanent state. In verse 9, Paul uses what is known as the aorist tense, which indicates a past event that has ongoing consequences. Since we have been justified (past event) we have peace with God (present experience). Having been put right and welcomed into the family, God will no more turn against us than against his only begotten son, Jesus!

So how does God feel when he looks at you? Not a frown of disappointment but a smile of joy. This is true whether we feel it or not, because it is not a mood based on our behaviour but a formal declaration, signed in the blood of Jesus. This is a solid foundation for living with peace. There is no greater person who could love you and rejoice over you than the one who already does! Almighty God has declared peace with us forever, so what do we have to fear?

Access to God

THROUGH [CHRIST] WE HAVE GAINED
ACCESS BY FAITH INTO THIS GRACE
IN WHICH WE NOW STAND.
Romans 5:2

Imagine a child grew up hating their parents before leaving home. They then became even more hostile so the parents had the locks changed to prevent further damage. But they never stopped loving their child. Now imagine that, one day, the child phones them and asks for forgiveness. The parents may forgive the child and make peace with them. But what next? They could decide that's as far as it goes. The air's cleared but the child must keep their distance. Alternatively, they might post a new set of keys with an invitation to come home.

That's the goal of salvation. It's full reconciliation with God. If we reduce it to just being let off the hook, we might spend the rest of our lives keeping our distance. In the story of the prodigal son, the rebellious child ends up back in the father's embrace, wearing a robe of purity and a ring of dignity. Justification sets up reconciliation. God our father wants us to come home.

Romans 5:2 affirms that 'we have gained access into this grace'. The Greek word for 'access' conveys the idea of being 'brought near' to someone powerful because someone else has made the introduction. A few years ago, my family and I visited the White House in Washington. In our case, we walked past the tourists taking photos behind the barrier, cleared security and entered the West Wing. How? Because a relative worked as a special assistant to the president. Her access gave us access, right through to the Oval Office. However, despite trying to persuade security with my 'cute' British accent, we could only peer through the doorway into the most powerful room in the world. I was disappointed. I wanted a photo behind the famous desk. But as we walked away, I felt the Holy Spirit whisper to me, 'Cheer up! I give you access to a far more powerful person every day!'

May we never lose the wonder of the access we have. Unlike Old Testament pilgrims, we don't have to travel to a holy building, offer animal sacrifices or watch priests entering the temple on our behalf. Through the blood of Jesus, we come straight through to God. We have the keys. We can enter freely and receive fresh grace on a daily basis. So don't let guilt or shame keep you away. Regardless of how you feel, God loves you. He's made peace with you. You have access to his presence.

In verse 8, Paul reminds us of the basis of all this: 'But God demonstrates his own love for us in this: while we were still sinners, Christ died for us'. This is one of my favourite verses in Romans. Why not commit it to memory so you can remind yourself of it regularly? Let's look at each phrase briefly:

'God demonstrates'

Talk is cheap and romantic love can be fickle. But God's love is not a sentimental mood. It is a determined decision, which has legs and arms. In real space and time, God *demonstrated* his passion for us.

'his own love'

The Greek dictionary had more options for 'love' than English. Paul could have chosen another word, such as *eros, philia* or *storge*. But instead, he drew on a relatively rare Greek word

– *agape* – which the early Christians adopted to convey the sacrificial nature of God's love. *Agape* holds nothing back. Agape bleeds and dies.

'while we were still sinners'

In verse 6 Paul describes us as 'powerless' and 'ungodly'. In other words, God showed his love for us while we were at our worst, not our best. So nothing can put him off now. You may attract someone to you by looking your best for a formal date. But what if they find out what you're really like? Will they still love you if you put on weight, lose your job or face long-term illness? This is the beauty of God's love. When we had nothing to offer him and no way to impress him, he loved us. Nothing can separate us from the love of God.

'Christ died for us'

A single event in history has defined the love of God for eternity. God's love is visceral and bloody. It is etched in space and time. On a rocky outcrop called Golgotha, outside the city walls of Jerusalem, the Son of God was brutally crucified. Why? Christ died for us because God loves us. If you want to know how much, look no further. As St Augustine famously noted, God loves each one of us as if there was only one of us to love. Romans chapter 5 invites us to sit down and rest at the foot of the cross. Here, God demonstrated his love for us. Here the prince of glory died for us. Take a moment to pause and reflect. Rest your tired legs and weary soul awhile. Take in the extraordinary view of God's *agape* love.

REFLECT: Which of the following phrases from Romans 5 do you most need to take on board for yourself? Why not insert your own name to make it personal?

_____ has 'been justified by faith'.
_____ has 'peace with God'.
_____ has been given 'access to grace'.
'God demonstrates his own love for _____.'
'While we were still sinners, Christ died for _____.'

◯◯ Part 2: God's peace is a lived experience

READ: Romans 5:12–21

If we are to enjoy a relationship with God, we need to be confident that he loves us in ways that are both formal and personal, past and present, facts and feelings.

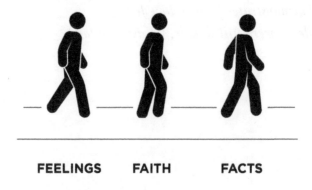

FEELINGS   FAITH   FACTS

Imagine three friends walking along a narrow path: 'Faith', 'Facts' and 'Feelings'. If Facts should take the lead, he can show Faith the way and Feelings will follow on behind. But if Faith starts worrying about how Feelings is doing and looks anxiously behind, Faith will start to wobble and fall off the path. Faith must keep their eyes on the Facts.

In part 1 of this chapter, we considered the objective truth of God's love. According to Paul, we have been justified (fact), we have peace with God (fact), we have access to God (fact), Christ died for us (fact), God demonstrated his love for us (fact). Our faith will become more confident and assured if we keep our eyes on these unchanging facts. The dangerous alternative is that we emphasise spiritual experiences and worry about feelings to such an extent that our theology becomes sentimental and we are easily swayed by doubts. If faith is not based on facts, we will be especially vulnerable to despair when tough times hit.

In Romans 5, Paul therefore blends past-tense description of the facts with present-tense references to a lived experience of God's love. Three times he says, 'We rejoice!' – in our hope 5:2, in our sufferings 5:3 and in God 5:11 (ESV UK). He describes in striking terms the profound experience of God's love being poured into our hearts by the Holy Spirit. While Christianity is based on facts, to say it doesn't include feelings is like the dentist getting the drill out and saying, 'Don't worry, you won't feel a thing!' When faith neglects the facts, it becomes *sentimental*, but the opposite danger is that our faith remains *theoretical* – a dry, sterile set of beliefs and religious exercises. If God's love does not travel from our heads to our hearts, other passions, relationships and interests will quickly become more appealing. Like a marriage relationship, mere duty and formality are never enough. True Christianity should also stir our emotions and desires.

In part 2 of this chapter, we look through Romans 5 to see what life looks like when viewed through the lens of God's love. Our relationship with God is much more than a covenant treaty. In addition to objective facts (*God loves everyone*), we can experience the personal reality: *God loves me!* This is when our personal assurance really moves to the right.

We experience God's love through suffering

> MORE THAN THAT, WE REJOICE IN
> OUR SUFFERINGS, KNOWING THAT
> SUFFERING PRODUCES ENDURANCE, AND
> ENDURANCE PRODUCES CHARACTER
> AND CHARACTER PRODUCES HOPE.
> Romans 5:3–4 (ESV UK)

In these verses, Paul considers the sort of peace we can have even in tough times. To be a Christian is not to avoid suffering but to experience it differently: 'we rejoice in our suffering' (5:3, ESV UK). What might this mean? If we haven't grasped the unchanging truth of God's love, when something bad happens we start to question everything at a deeper level: *What have I done wrong? Why is God angry? Doesn't he love me any more?* These doubts add a layer of depression onto what was already a tough set of circumstances. But if we grasp the unchanging nature of God's love – *I am justified in Christ. I have peace with God. I can access his grace any time. He is for me not against me* – then we can keep our eyes on the facts. Even in the storms, we can remain hopeful. In fact, our hearts may 'rejoice' in God's love and experience his peace more profoundly because of the trials.

Recently, I went mountain climbing in the Swiss Alps with my son. As we made our way up through alpine pastures on a lovely sunny day, Joel charged off full of confidence. However, the gradient soon changed and we found ourselves committed to a more challenging route than we'd expected. We both became silent with concentration. Then we heard a rumble of thunder as storm clouds began to billow around us. So I got the rope out and made sure Joel was tied to me and stayed close. Fortunately, the storm moved away, the sun came out and we made it to the summit.

Of all our adventures, that is the one Joel refers to the most. There we bonded together and came through adversity. This is Paul's point. Suffering takes our faith beyond theory. It's a lived experience of trusting in God's loving care. As we go through life's storms, we draw closer to God. False hopes and vain distractions fall away. Secure in God's unchanging *agape* love, we can rejoice even through suffering.

That said, some experiences of suffering may feel like unbearable loss, violent storm clouds without any silver lining. I recently spent time with leaders from different African nations. One couple told me about a widow they had been supporting in their home country in West Africa. Her husband had been a faithful pastor, serving the local community for several years. However, one day, Muslim extremists came to the village and issued a warning: 'If you are still here when we come back, we will kill you.'

Her husband refused to leave the place to which God had called him. Then, one Sunday, at the end of the service, the extremists returned and killed her husband while members of the congregation fled for their lives. What can you say to that? It's unimaginable persecution and loss. However, the couple told me that through it all, the widow was finding comfort from the fact that God knows the pain of suffering because of the cross and that in the end he will restore what we have lost. This is what we have to hold on to when the storm clouds roll in.

In Romans 5, Paul also highlights character development as a positive outcome when we face tough times. This may seem counter-intuitive to us. Suffering normally suggests weakness and defeat. However, faith is like a muscle; it will weaken when it is not used. But when we respond to hardship by trusting God more deeply, it produces greater resilience and strength. If we learn to face testing times secure in God's love, we can become confident, all-weather Christians, unshaken by outer circumstances.

When I was growing up, one of my favourite comedians was Peter Kay. As a northerner, he was well trained at dunking a biscuit in a mug of tea. On one of his shows, he captured the devastating moment when a weak biscuit is overwhelmed by the heat and collapses into your mug. By contrast, he suggests, Hobnob biscuits are made of sturdier stuff. They are so resilient they can take a good dunking and still come back for more! So, it is with faith: if we are to become resilient Christians, the key is not in being brave types who win medals. What makes the difference is that we are secure in God's unchanging love. Then, instead of giving way in the heat, we can live out the truth that 'suffering produces perseverance'.

We experience God's love by the Holy Spirit

> HOPE DOES NOT PUT US TO SHAME,
> BECAUSE GOD'S LOVE HAS BEEN POURED
> OUT INTO OUR HEARTS THROUGH THE HOLY
> SPIRIT, WHO HAS BEEN GIVEN TO US.
> Romans 5:5

In this beautiful verse, Paul refers to an intimate experience of God's love through the Holy Spirit. Though he uses the past tense in verse 5, this experience is available to us on an ongoing basis. God's love does not fluctuate or change, but our emotions do. Like a balloon, our hearts can become deflated. But equally, they can expand to new capacities and take in more of God's love. For Paul, the love of God is therefore a historic event – 'Christ died for us' (5:8) – and a present experience. The Holy Spirit enables us to personally experience the very love that Jesus had when he died on the cross all those years ago. The depth and quality of God's *agape* love have not changed since then. His heart is still white-hot with passion for us. It is the regular ministry of the Holy Spirit to help us know it and feel it for ourselves.

AS A RESULT OF BEING JUSTIFIED BY FAITH . . .
WE ARE SURROUNDED BY GOD'S LOVE AND
GENEROSITY, INVITED TO BREATHE IT IN AS
OUR NATIVE AIR . . . THIS IS WHAT TRULY
HUMAN EXISTENCE OUGHT TO BE LIKE
AND IT IS THE BEGINNING OF SOMETHING
SO BIG, SO MASSIVE, SO UNIMAGINABLY
BEAUTIFUL AND POWERFUL, THAT WE
ALMOST BURST AS WE THINK OF IT.

N. T. Wright[2]

I remember when I first experienced God's love in a profoundly personal way. I physically felt a warm sensation as God's love filled me from head to toe. I remember saying over and over in front of my youth leader who had been praying for me, '*God* loves me! God *loves* me! God loves *me*!' As I repeated the same short sentence, the emphasis kept changing as my spiritual lungs breathed in more and more of God's love. This experience gave me a deep assurance of God's love that has remained a constant through life's ups and downs.

John Wesley (1703–91), co-founder of the Methodist movement, famously experienced God's love in London during the eighteenth century. Wesley had become extremely devout and religious while studying at Oxford University. He was part of a group nicknamed the 'Holy Club' and went to America as a missionary in his zeal to serve God. However, in a fierce storm on board a ship, Wesley became terrified of dying and bemoaned his lack of assurance: 'I went to America to convert the Indians. But who will convert me?' Back in London, he attended a Christian meeting in a building located on the site where the Barbican now stands. In his journal, he recorded what happened on that day, 24 May 1738. Note the way Romans features once again:

> In the evening I went very unwillingly to a society in Aldersgate Street, where one was reading [Martin] Luther's preface to the Epistle to the Romans. About a quarter before nine, while he was describing the change, which God works in the heart through faith in Christ, I felt my heart strangely warmed. I felt I did trust in Christ, Christ alone, for salvation; and an assurance was given me that He had taken away my sins, even mine.[3]

This experience of God's love was a game-changer. It may not have seemed dramatic if you'd been standing next to John Wesley at the time. But when the Spirit pours God's love into our hearts, something comes alive, like a fire in the hearth. Wesley went on to serve Christ with unceasing energy and left a legacy of renewed faith in the United Kingdom and beyond. The key to his joyful resilience was a new assurance: God loves *me*!

Throughout Romans we have been climbing steadily higher. Now we can see more clearly how the Holy Spirit helps us to personally experience salvation. We are deeply loved. We have peace with God and open access to him. Whatever life throws at us, nothing can separate us from God's love. On our adventure through Paul's letter, we have reached a new high point. For me, Romans 5 is the most beautiful view yet. Here we can rest in the truth that 'having been justified by faith, we have peace with God' (5:1). Here we can experience the unconditional and unchanging love of God through the Holy Spirit. Breathe it in like fresh lugs of mountain air.

REFLECT: Pray over Romans 5:5. Ask God to fill you with his Spirit and to give you a personal experience of his love and peace. Why not do this once a day for the next week?

> God demonstrates his own love for us in this: while we were still sinners, Christ died for us.
>
> *Romans 5:8*

5

The ridge of freedom

Romans 6:1—7:25

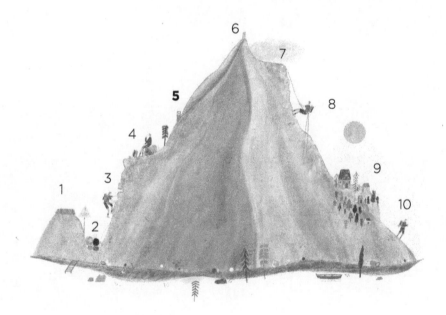

The edge of freedom

Romans 6:14-23

The drug dealer parked outside the gym, took a gun out of the glove compartment and waited. Someone was about to learn the hard way that gang culture can be ruthless. As the gym door opened, Mick got out of the car, his finger fidgeting on the trigger. But the target was not alone. Two young children walked beside him. Suddenly, a piercing light came from one of them and blinded Mick on the spot. He staggered back to the car, shaking with fear. As he sat there, contemplating suicide, a phrase leapt into his consciousness: 'The wages of sin is death.' Where did that come from? A forgotten Bible verse from childhood days – Romans 6:23. The gun went back into the glove compartment. The family went home, blissfully unaware that an act of God had just saved their lives.

I know about this incident, because years later I was lecturing at a theological college near Manchester. After class had finished, a kind student offered me a lift to the train station. On the way, I asked him how he had become a Christian and why he was now training for ordination. The former gang member told me a story that I would never forget. By the time we got to the station, I was relieved to get out in one piece! Months later I was moved to tears when I saw 'Pastor Mick' meeting Prince

William and being interviewed on national news. Transformed by the gospel, the former drug dealer is now helping the most vulnerable in Burnley.[1]

Paul opened his letter to the Romans with a bold claim: the gospel is 'the power of God that brings salvation' (1:16). Nothing has changed. The same light that blinded Saul on the road to Damascus can still dazzle drug dealers in the twenty-first century. The gospel transforms people in such a radical way that the best analogy to capture the change is *death and resurrection*.

However, no sooner have I said that than other stories come to mind. I think of 'Tony', for example. After putting his faith in Christ, he struggled to change. Despite hours of counselling and even some prayer ministry, he remained stuck in sinful patterns of lust, envy and self-pity. He once described his experience like holding on to Jesus through prison bars while still feeling trapped inside. If the gospel is so powerful, why can Christians still feel trapped in cycles of sin? If God's purpose for our lives is freedom, what are some of us missing?

In this chapter we consider Romans 6:1–7:25. Here, Paul reveals how the gospel enables us to 'live a new life' (6:4). The work of Jesus Christ is not limited to forgiveness. The gospel brings true freedom. However, Romans 7 also contains some gritty verses that articulate feelings of frustration, which many of us will resonate with: 'I do not do the good I want to do, but the evil I do not want to do . . . What a wretched man I am!' (Rom. 7:19, 24). Do you ever find yourself determined not to do something but then doing it anyway? If Romans 6 is a celebration of Christian *freedom*, Romans 7 is an outburst of *frustration*. Together, these chapters help balance the reality of the gospel in a fallen world – real progress but moments of regress, the power to change but the lure of temptation, the transformation of Mick and the frustration of Tony. As we ascend towards the summit peak of Romans, we need to hold both these realities in tension. Change is a work of grace and a steady climb, one step at a time.

For me, one of the most exhilarating experiences is moving along a narrow and exposed ridge. The lower sections of a mountain are often broad and ill-defined. But high ridges are dramatic, with steep cliffs falling away on either side. Some of the best scrambles in Britain include arêtes like Crib Goch on Snowdon (Wales), Striding Edge on Helvellyn (England) and, my favourite, the Cullin Ridge on Skye (Scotland). It's so narrow in places you must move along as though on horseback, one leg either side!

I love narrow arêtes because they are so defined. The way forward could not be clearer. I've entitled this chapter on Romans 6—7 *the ridge of freedom*. Up to this point, Paul's argument has been broad and expansive. But this section narrows down, with more detailed instructions on what we must do. There is no room for wandering off course. Either side there are dangers to be avoided. In the Bible, this is what true freedom feels like. As Jesus himself said, the 'narrow' way leads to eternal life but the 'broad' way of popular choice leads to destruction (see Matthew 7:13–14). Freedom is not found in wandering wherever we please. Instead, as we follow the narrow way, we will experience greater liberation and become the people we were made to be.

 Part 1: Know it

In Romans 6:1–11, Paul unpacks how we should see ourselves in order to live in freedom. Most Christians know that *Christ died for them*, but do we know that *we died with Christ*?

○─○ Part 2: Live it!

In Romans 6:12–14, Paul gets practical about applying what we *know* to how we *live*. As God's people, we can exercise our freedom by refusing to give sin any opportunity.

> Offer yourselves to God as those who have been brought from death to life . . . sin shall no longer be your master.
>
> *Romans 6:13–14*

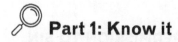

Part 1: Know it

READ: Romans 6:1–23

So far, Paul has led us down into *the valley of sin* (chapters 1—2), then guided us through *the crux of salvation* (chapter 3), before following the footsteps of Abraham (chapter 4) that brought us to a beautiful viewpoint (chapter 5). There we paused to take in the love of God as both a historic event and a profound experience. Our salvation is completely secured in Christ, and nothing can separate us from God's love. It's not based on my moral performance but on Christ's righteousness. Even my sin – past, present and future – cannot disrupt the peace treaty that has been signed in his blood.

When we put it like that, it sounds too good to be true, don't you think? It's not uncommon at this point to experience a form of spiritual vertigo that leaves us feeling a bit light-headed. New thoughts may begin to surface in your mind that seem tempting: *If, according to Romans 1—5, salvation is sorted regardless of my sin, does it really matter if I go on sinning? If I am forgiven no matter what, what's the harm in a few guilty pleasures?* Should similar thoughts flash into your mind, take heart. It means we've followed the contours of Paul's argument and arrived at the very question that he briefly entertains: 'What shall we say, then? Shall we go on sinning so that grace may increase?' (6:1).

In posing this dilemma, Paul is double-checking that we've grasped the radical implications of God's grace. Salvation is not a match-funded scheme – we put some good in and God will make up the rest. It's a free gift that we never have to pay back. When we really grasp this truth, it can imply a rather tempting formula:

SALVATION BY GRACE = PERMISSION TO SIN

If grace is seen most clearly when we sin, might our failure even provide an opportunity for God to show what he can do? I remember a friend who was in the police force telling me about an arrest he made for domestic violence. As he handcuffed the man, his partner trembling in the other room, the abuser said, 'You should be grateful. I'm keeping you in a job.' That sick thought contains a measure of truth. If all crime ceased, my friend would have to find a new career. But what a twisted way of seeing the world – domestic violence as a form of job creation. Paul feels the same about any notion that our sin is keeping Jesus in a job.

Having teed up the provocative question ('Shall we go on sinning?'), Paul gives an emphatic response: 'By no means!' (NIVUK), 'Certainly not' (NKJV), 'What a ghastly thought' (J. B. Phillips).[2] If we confuse grace with a cheap excuse, we reduce it to something like an insurance policy. This only reveals how little we've understood about true freedom. It's not just *freedom from* living in sin but also *freedom to* serve Christ: *Paulos doulos* (1:1 'Paul, a servant'), remember? Justification by faith should lead to a life that embodies the very righteousness we first receive as a gift.

The rest of Romans 6 explains how this freedom works in two main stages. First, we need to know who we are *theologically*, and then we need to live it out *practically*.

DON'T YOU KNOW THAT ALL OF US WHO WERE
BAPTISED INTO CHRIST JESUS WERE BAPTISED
INTO HIS DEATH? WE WERE THEREFORE BURIED
WITH HIM THROUGH BAPTISM INTO DEATH
IN ORDER THAT, JUST AS CHRIST WAS RAISED
FROM THE DEAD THROUGH THE GLORY OF
THE FATHER, WE TOO MAY LIVE A NEW LIFE.

Romans 6:3–4

When Paul wants to help people change, he turns to something
we need to *know* before anything we need to *do*. The whole of
Romans is structured this way. The first eleven chapters are
almost entirely taken up with what God has done and what it
means for us. Only after a sustained focus on belief-change
does Paul finally turn to something resembling behaviour-
change.

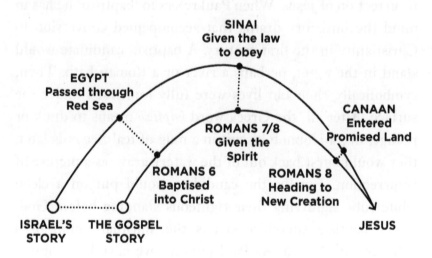

How the Gospel story fulfills Israel's story

In Romans 6—8, Paul deliberately echoes the story of Israel's
Exodus in order to illustrate how Christian freedom works.

When they were trapped as slaves under Pharaoh, a Passover Lamb was sacrificed and its blood brought them deliverance. Then, when they were trapped between Pharaoh's army and the Red Sea, Moses simply declared, 'Stand still, and see the salvation of the LORD' (Exod. 14:13, NKJV). As they passed through the divided waters of the Red Sea, they were experiencing the truth that salvation is a gift. However, once on the other side, Israel had to learn how to live out the freedom they had been given. Instead of seeing themselves as slaves to Pharaoh, they needed to embrace their new identity as freed people and live it out in practical ways. This idea is reflected in the teaching of Jesus who declared, 'know the truth, and the truth will set you free' (John 8:32).

So, what is it that we need to *know* in order to live out our *freedom*? In Romans 6, Paul highlights the fact that a Christian has been baptised or immersed into the death, burial and resurrection of Jesus. When Paul refers to 'baptism' he has in mind the initiatory drama that accompanied conversion to Christianity in the first century. A baptism candidate would stand in the water, perhaps a river or a Roman bath. Then, symbolically, their old lives were fully immersed under the surface. After all, the Greek word *baptizo* means to dunk or plunge, like a Hobnob biscuit in a mug of tea! Seconds later, they would burst back out of the watery grave as a picture of resurrection. Finally, the candidate would put on a clean white robe signifying their righteous standing before God. Water baptism therefore enacts the spiritual union of a believer with Christ. As Paul puts it, 'we have been united with him' (6:5). Remember the bookmark-inside-the-book illustration in the last chapter? We are 'in Christ'. Therefore, what happened to him – death, burial and resurrection – is now true of us.

With this in mind, Paul declares something truly radical: 'our old self was crucified with [Christ]' (6:6). Literally, Paul refers to us being co-crucified, co-buried and co-resurrected with Christ. Now, it seems to me that many Christians either don't *know* this or don't *own* it for themselves. We regularly affirm that Christ was *crucified for* us but what about the reversible truth – we were *crucified with* Christ? If the former truth guarantees our *forgiveness*, the latter is key to our *freedom*. When Christ died for my sin, my old self died with him. When he was buried, I was buried. When he was resurrected, I was raised to new life. My identity has been fundamentally altered through my union with Christ. I am no longer a sinner, enslaved to evil forces more powerful than me. I belong to God. As Paul concludes in verse 7, 'anyone who has died *has been set free* from sin' (italics added).

Notice that Paul affirms this truth for 'all' who are 'in Christ'. He is not describing an elite state of purity that we work towards over many years. It's an upfront status change that remains true regardless. You may not feel particularly dead to sin right now, but that's not the point. Isn't it perfectly possible for something to be true about you without you knowing it or feeling it? Your flies are undone, your car brake light isn't working or, more positively, a large sum of money has been deposited in your account. Having been blissfully unaware, you are so grateful to the person who pointed out what had been true all along. In Romans 6, Paul is pointing out that from the moment we believed in Jesus Christ we were united to him. We have therefore died to sin and been raised to new life, whether we realised it or not.

Here's another way to think of it. Do you believe that two thieves were crucified with Jesus? If so, on what basis? Probably you would say, 'Because the Bible says so.' Well, the same Bible says *you* were crucified with Jesus (Gal. 2.20). So we must not see ourselves as sinners doing our best to reform our ways. That's hopeless. The truth is far more dramatic than that. Our old self is dead and buried. The sooner we realise this, the sooner we can live in the good of it.

To illustrate the point, imagine slaves in Rome who were legally owned by a master. How could they hope to become free? Well, just suppose the slave died. That would instantly terminate their obligation to serve the master! This is Paul's point. Spiritually speaking, we died with Christ and that terminated any obligation to sin. Having been raised with him to new life on the other side, sin is no longer our master. Of course, that's not to say we *can't* sin. But we don't *have to*. In Christ, we are free.

Whether your story is more like Mick the assassin or Tony the struggling Christian, this is what we need to *know* in order to live out our freedom. Of course, it's important to be accountable to others, asking them to pray for us and not being afraid to share our struggles and failings. After all, as we saw in Romans 1—3, the gospel gives us permission to be honest and not to hide behind feelings of embarrassment or shame. However, Romans 6 also invites us to enter into the freedom that Christ has won for us by personally identifying with his death and resurrection.

If I'm honest, for many years I identified more with Tony's experience. As a Christian, I struggled with hidden sins that became cycles of behaviour. The more I gave in, the more I gave in. You get used to it. It's just the way it is, right? But when I came to understand Romans 6, it changed the way I thought about myself. For the first time, I owned the fact that I had died with Christ, my old life was buried and I had been raised with him. From then on, whenever I felt tempted to sin, I would affirm the truth, out loud if possible: *I have been crucified with Christ. I don't have to do this. It is not me any more. I am free to live a new life.* Knowing who we are is a game-changer. It's not mere make-believe or positive thinking. It's us catching up with what's already true. As *The Message* translation puts it:

> Our old way of life was nailed to the cross with Christ, a decisive end to that sin-miserable life – no longer captive to sin's demands!
>
> *Romans 6:6–7 (MSG)*

REFLECT: Read Romans 6:3–4. What does it mean to know that *you died with Christ* and have been set free from the control of sin? How might this change your perception of yourself?

◯ᴖ◯ Part 2: Live it!

READ: Romans 7:1–25

At the start of Romans 6, Paul addressed the danger of an anything-goes-moral-relativism: 'Shall we go on sinning? By no means!' In Romans 7, Paul deals with a danger that lurks on the other side of the narrow ridge of freedom – religious legalism. For an audience of Jewish converts, this would have been a particularly challenging section. While they agreed that faith in Jesus saves, isn't it keeping the law that leads to further progress? If a Christian wants to change, don't they need to keep the Ten Commandments and set their alarm clock earlier for more Bible and prayer? In Romans 7, Paul uses the metaphor of marriage to unpick this logic. He compares God's law to a husband to whom God's people were married under the old covenant. While this husband is not sinful – Paul affirms the law to be 'holy, righteous and good' (7:12) – the problem is that it cannot change us. All the law can do is reveal what is right and judge what is wrong.

The old covenant of law is a husband who's always right, tells us when we are wrong but never lifts a finger to help. (When my wife read the previous sentence, she nodded as if she knew the guy!) Trying to work harder to please this kind of husband will only lead to despair. Indeed, the final section of Romans 7 describes the frustration of someone under the law who wants to change but can't:

> For I know that good itself does not dwell in me, that is, in my sinful nature. For I have the desire to do what is good, but I cannot carry it out. For I do not do the good I want to do, but the evil I do not want to do – this I keep on doing . . . What a

wretched man I am! Who will rescue me from this body that is
subject to death?

Romans 7:18–19, 24

Much theological ink has been spilt trying to identify the
person behind this honest outburst. Most obviously it could be
Paul himself, struggling with sins he can't shake off. However,
this is problematic given that either side of this passage he cele-
brates the freedom we have as Christians (Rom. 6:1–14;
8:1–11).[3] Others have wondered whether Paul was giving voice
to how he used to feel in his pre-Christian days, living without
the power of the gospel. Or perhaps Paul was impersonating an
imaginary Jew or God-fearing Gentile who knows God's law
but cannot keep it because their 'sinful nature' holds them
back.[4]

Without wanting to sidestep an important debate that has
raged since Augustine of Hippo (fourth century AD), my own
view is that Paul left the 'I' deliberately ambiguous. He
wanted this passage to resonate with a whole range of audi-
ences. The cry of despair in 7:24 could belong to an honest
Jew reading the Torah, a devout Muslim fearing the justice of
Allah, a secular humanist who can't keep their New Year's
resolutions or a Christian who has allowed sin to reassert
control. For Paul, the key issue is that the law is powerless to
change us. Like a spirit level, God's commandments can show
us what is crooked, but they can't straighten us out. Trying to
find freedom through the law only breeds pride and a judgmental spirit if we think we are succeeding, and then condemnation and despair when we inevitably fail. Therefore, Romans
7 is clear that as well as putting sin to death, Christ has ended
our relationship to the law.

So, my brothers and sisters, you also died to the law through the body of Christ, that you might belong to another, to him who was raised from the dead, in order that we might bear fruit for God.

Romans 7:4

Today, Christians can still slip into a legalistic mindset. Having been justified by Jesus, we try to make progress through a list of spiritual dos and don'ts – go to church, read the Bible, tithe your salary (before tax), quit smoking, stop drinking and block porn. These are all good goals, but they can easily become a joyless religion of law and duty.

> RUN, JOHN, AND WORK, THE LAW COMMANDS,
> YET FINDS ME NEITHER FEET NOR HANDS,
> BUT SWEETER NEWS THE GOSPEL BRINGS,
> IT BIDS ME FLY AND LENDS ME WINGS!
> John Berridge, hymn writer (1716–93)[5]

So how can we 'bear fruit for God' in a way that is truly liberating? Well, we need to follow the narrow ridge of freedom and not fall into either moral liberalism on the one side – freedom is going my own way – or religious legalism on the other side – freedom is obeying the law. With this in mind, let's return to Paul's argument in Romans chapter 6, which goes on to highlight three principles that guide us along the ridge of freedom.

6:11: 'Count yourselves dead to sin'

Here, Paul draws on an accounting term – 'count' or 'reckon' – in order to underline the importance of knowing what's true regardless of how we feel. We need to get our accounts in order, put the sums in the right column and do the maths! We are dead to sin and alive to God. Count on it. Bank it. Live in the good of it. It's as if Paul is sitting us down and saying, 'Take a good look at what is now yours in Christ. Let it inspire you to live a new life.' Whether we feel it or not, Christ's victory over sin is ours.

A famous preacher from the twentieth century, Dr Martyn Lloyd-Jones, taught through Romans in painstaking detail – it took him twelve years to finish! In one lecture, he used a helpful illustration about the importance of counting ourselves free.

Take the case of those poor slaves in the United States of America about a hundred years ago. There they were in a condition of slavery. Then the American Civil War came, and as the result of that war, slavery was abolished in the United States. But what had actually happened? All slaves, young and old, were given their freedom, but many of the older ones who had endured long years of servitude found it very difficult to understand their new status. They heard the announcement that slavery was abolished and that they were free: but hundreds, not to say thousands, of times in their after-lives and experiences many of them did not realize it, and when they saw their old master coming near them they began to quake and to tremble, and to wonder whether they were going to be sold . . . You can still be a slave experientially, even when you are no longer a slave legally . . . Whatever you may feel, whatever your experience may be, God tells us here, through his word, that if we are in Christ we are no longer . . . under the reign and rule of sin . . . if I fall into sin, as I do, it is simply because I do not realize who I am . . . Realize it! Reckon it![6]

Isn't that challenging? You can still be a slave experientially, even though you have been set free legally. This is Paul's point. Before we were Christians, when we chose to sin, we were doing what came naturally. As slaves, we were trapped in cycles that we could not break free from. In a sense, we had to sin. But now we have a new master. So if as a Christian I want to sin, I still can. But I don't have to. When I sin, it's like turning up at my old place of work but this time as a volunteer. I'm serving my old boss again even though I don't work there. Paul is saying, 'Why would you? I mean, what good has sin ever done you? If we have been set free, why go back?'

Instead, Paul says, 'Count yourselves dead to sin' (6:11). Catch up with what's true about you now and live it. If a former slave is legally free, it doesn't matter how much their former master shouts at them. They are free to walk away. This remains true, even when we give in to temptation and return briefly to our old ways. Just because we sin occasionally, this doesn't make us sinners again. No, we are still made righteous in Christ. All is not lost. So let's close the gap between slipping back into sin and returning to Christ in repentance. You don't have to stay at a distance and make up for it by some kind of spiritual time out. Instead, we can return to our true master who will never condemn us. To live in freedom, we must do the maths: *I have died to sin. I am alive to God. Sin is not my master. I am free in Christ!*

6:13: 'Do not offer any part of yourself to sin'

With our new status clear, Paul moves into command mode: 'Therefore do not let sin reign in your mortal body' (6:12). You might be wondering at this point why, if we have died to sin, is there still a risk it might 'reign' in us? But notice Paul is careful to qualify his concern with the phrase 'in your mortal body'.

Paul's theology affirms that our bodies (Greek *soma*) were created good but they have become corrupted by our 'sinful nature' (Greek *sarx*). Our *bodies* do not yet share in Christ's risen life. While spiritually we are united with Christ and freed from sin, physically, mentally and emotionally we are still prone to temptation, lies and disordered desires. At the risk of being simplistic, our spiritual *software* may have been upgraded but our *hardware* is the same old kit, still prone to malfunction. As we will see in the next chapter, one day our bodies will be redeemed beyond any possibility of sin (Rom. 8:23). But in the meantime, we should not be surprised that sinful thoughts and desires still tempt us. The struggles we experience are because in Christ we are *new creations* (2 Cor. 5:17) and yet we still inhabit this *old creation*.

For this reason, Paul tells people to fight against sinful desires. He refers to our body as an 'instrument' (6:13) and urges us not to offer any part to sin. It's a powerful idea. Our bodies can make melody to the glory of God or they can be played out of tune by sin. For example, we can use our tongues to tell crude jokes, lie about achievements or gossip about others, or we can control our tongue so it becomes an instrument of goodness and truth. Equally, we have a God-given sex drive and attraction towards others. We can allow sin to co-opt such desires so our bodies become instruments of lust, envy and shame, or we can refuse to act on impure thoughts. After all, Jesus Christ was crucified to deliver us from the power of sin. More than that, we were crucified with him. So temptation and sinful desires do not have to push us off the ridge of freedom.

We used to live in a house near the sea in Cornwall. After a while, we moved to another property about a mile away. For the first few weeks, I would find myself driving back to the old house on automatic pilot. On one occasion I actually pulled up on the driveway before it occurred to me, 'I don't live here any more!' I quickly put the car in reverse and drove home. In the same way, we can find our bodies and minds taking us back to old patterns, habits and ways of relating to others. But when sin tempts us to revisit our old ways, we can declare, 'I am in Christ. That's not how I live any more. My new home is righteousness!' Practically, this means putting some distance between ourselves and sin so we can't just wander back into old ways on automatic pilot. We can install software to block unhelpful content on our screens, make ourselves accountable to others, refuse to work late with someone we find attractive. Whatever it takes, even if we have to cut ties, the important thing is that you 'do not let sin reign in your mortal body' (6:12).

6:13: 'Offer yourselves to God'

Finally, Paul urges us to positively pursue life as God's servants. Too often, Christians are known for what we are against. Instead, Paul is passionate about how we can become 'instruments of righteousness' (6:13). As a boy, I remember my mother whispering repeatedly to me in church, 'Sit still and be good!' I couldn't manage it for a minute. Fortunately, that's not what God is whispering to his people. Idle hands make for the devil's work. Instead, we are to serve God with our wallets, tongues, abilities and time. This is how we recover from the dehumanising effects of sin and become the people we were made to be. As St Augustine concluded, God is the master whom to serve is perfect freedom.[7] This is a great paradox. Many people think that if they serve God, they will lose their freedom. In fact, the opposite is true. Living for ourselves is a form of slavery. Serving God 'in the new way of the Spirit' (Rom. 7:6) is true freedom.

Once again, I think Paul has Israel's Exodus in mind. When God parted the Red Sea, they passed through a corridor of water, a bit like baptism. Once they came out the other side, the waters closed over and cut them off from Pharaoh's control. All of a sudden, these Israelites were no longer slaves. Their metaphorical death to Egypt and resurrection on the other side ended any obligation. So it is with a Christian who has been united with Jesus Christ. We are no longer slaves to sin. We have crossed over to the other side. Now we are called to be servants of God. This is true freedom – it's not just coming out from oppression (Egypt); it's entering into the Promised Land of purity and honour.

This is the beautiful ridge of freedom that leads all the way to the summit. To follow it requires giving up wrong attitudes, bad habits and hidden sins. This can be tough. But the freedom we experience in Christ is so worth it. Equally, there may be moments when we fall along the way. Like Tony, we may even despair of hope. However, I urge us not to give in to feelings of condemnation. Instead, we can embrace the teaching of Romans 6—7: *know it* ('count yourself dead to sin'), *live it* ('offer yourselves to God').

Have you now grasped this vision for yourself? Imagine the difference it could make to really know that we are freed from the power of sin. As we conclude this section of Romans, take a moment to reflect on what it might mean to personally own these liberating truths and to put them into practice:

You are dead to sin and alive to God. That's what Jesus did.

That means you must not give sin a vote in the way you conduct your lives. Don't give it the time of day. Don't even run little errands that are connected with that old way of life. Throw yourselves wholeheartedly and full-time . . . into God's way of doing things. Sin can't tell you how to live. After all, you're not living under that old tyranny any longer. You're living in the freedom of God.

Romans 6:11–14 (MSG)

REFLECT: Consider verses 12–14 and make a note of any feelings or thoughts that flood your mind. Bring them to God and ask him to help you walk in the freedom that Jesus has secured for us.

> Offer yourselves to God as those who have been brought from death to life . . . sin shall no longer be your master.
>
> *Romans 6:13–14*

6

The summit of hope

Romans 8:1-39

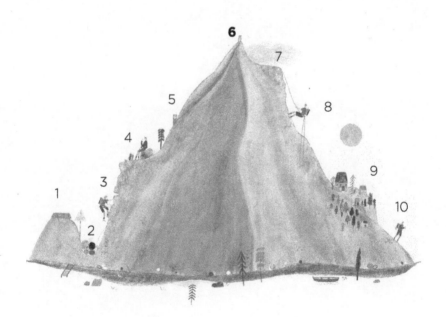

Something strange happens when you reach the summit of a big mountain. For what seems like forever you've been toiling upwards, straining into a steep slope. Then suddenly, the ground falls away in front of your feet and the horizon bursts open. You stagger around, elated, taking in the view. Whole vistas that were previously out of sight now reveal themselves: *Look down there. That's where we started . . . Wow, is that Ben Nevis in the distance? That must be the Isle of Skye over there!*

As Paul dictated Romans, I think summit-fever took over when he reached chapter 8. As we'll see, it lasts to the end of chapter 11, which is why he opens chapter 12 with the phrase, 'Therefore . . . *in view* of God's mercy . . .' (12:1, italics added). The preceding chapters have brought us to a high point, where we get to take in the amazing 'view'. Romans 8 is in many ways the peak of the letter. For me, there's no better vantage point in the whole Bible.

Remember, Romans 6—7 was a narrow ridge of freedom that demanded careful focus. But Romans 8 is different. From here, magnificent views open up in every direction. I like to imagine Paul spinning round and pointing excitedly: *Look where we've come from ... There's no condemnation in Christ Jesus! Now, you can see the Spirit at work. He makes us God's children! And look, over there in the distance, the ultimate Promised Land!* Romans 8 is a 360-degree panorama of God's great purpose, from the dawn of time and into eternity. Paul's breadth of vision helps to reframe our small, brief existence in the light of something much grander and more significant. It gives us confidence to face the future, knowing God's purpose will prevail. This is absolutely foundational to the Gospel. As Paul puts it, 'in this hope we were saved' (8:24).

> ROMANS CHAPTER EIGHT IS A PILLOW ON
> WHICH TO REST OUR WEARY HEADS.
> John Stott[1]

I believe our fragile, anxious culture needs Romans 8 more than ever. The secular worldview, which dominates Western society, has rejected any overarching plotline to life. As a result, horizons have collapsed and imaginations shrivelled. The entire meaning of life can be reduced to seeking pleasure, status and comfort before we die. No wonder we are facing a social pandemic of anxiety, loneliness and disillusionment. To live with peace, we need to be anchored to a larger narrative. To live with confidence, we need a hope that even suffering and death cannot snatch away. So don't just read Romans 8. It's far too important for that. Memorise it, meditate on it and marinate your soul in it!

Part 1: The big picture

From the vantage point of Romans 8, Paul looks back to our *past* and declares 'no condemnation', then he considers how secure we are in the *present* as God's children before finally looking ahead to a *future* hope of resurrection and new creation.

⊙⊙ Part 2: God is for us

Paul reflects on how our eternal hope makes us 'more than conquerors' (8:37). By the way, part 1 is much longer than part 2 because I got carried away with the view!

> We wait eagerly for our adoption to sonship, the redemption of our bodies. For in this hope we were saved.
>
> *Romans 8:23–4*

Part 1: The big picture

READ: Romans 8:1–30

In Romans 8:1–30, Paul points in three different directions to capture the way the gospel relates to our past, present and future. Each perspective can be summarised by a key theological word. The first is 'justification' and it relates to our past.

Justification > Adoption > Glorification
(8:1-11)   (8:12-17)   (8:18-30)

The word 'therefore' (8:1) casts our minds back to the preceding passage. Do you remember that tormented soul in Romans 7, who knows God's law but cannot keep it? *Why do we love the things that hurt us and hurt those who love us?* Chapter 7 concluded with an agonising cry: 'What a wretched man I am! Who will rescue me?' (7:24). Paul's 'therefore' in Romans 8 is a direct response to this cry for help. In effect, the bridge between Romans 7 and 8 goes something like this: *For all those who feel hopeless, trapped in cycles of failure, I've got good news: 'There is now no condemnation for those who are in Christ Jesus!'* If Paul had said this back in Romans 5 it might have referred primarily to forgiveness. However, we are higher up now and able to see the bigger picture. The gospel is more than a detergent to shift guilty stains. It is also a jailbreak from the dominion of sin. Not only did Christ die for us (forgiveness), but we also died with Christ (freedom). By chapter 8, we can therefore interpret Paul's teaching in the fullest sense – we are not condemned under the penalty of sin *and* we are no longer ruled by the power of sin. There is no condemnation.

I remember pulling into a train station and seeing some rusty old wagons lined up in a siding, waiting to be melted down. On each was painted in rough letters, 'condemned'. It's easy to live as if something similar is graffitied over our lives. After all, we have a record that is more than enough to condemn us and we have a real spiritual enemy who loves to accuse us. If we are not careful, we will believe what we should doubt (condemning thoughts) and doubt what we should believe (gospel truth).

Perhaps you are familiar with feelings of condemnation? At different times I've had to wrestle with some of the following doubts and fears. Are any of them troubling you right now?

- Fearing the worst: *What if my past secrets catch up with me?*
- Doubting God's love when tough times hit: *Is this God punishing me?*
- Not feeling good enough or forgiven: *I must try harder to make up for it . . .*
- Wearing a super-spiritual mask: *I must try to impress God and other people.*
- Fear of failure and responsibility: *God can't use me. I'll just muck it up . . .*

As we've seen, the gospel includes a legal declaration of acquittal – a 'not guilty' verdict. In Romans 8, Paul reminds us of the basis for this great hope: 'God [sent] his own Son *in the likeness* of sinful flesh to be a sin offering' (8:3, italics added). These carefully chosen words underscore that Jesus was truly human like us and yet was not tainted by sin. He stood in our shoes but never made our mistakes. Then, on the cross, Jesus became a 'sin offering'. Body and blood, soul and spirit, he took our guilt and shame and 'condemned sin in the flesh' (8:3).

Don't miss the word play here. Because Jesus was condemned (past), there is now 'no condemnation' for us (present). God has not swept our sin under the carpet, with the possibility it might surface again. He nailed it to the cross until justice was fully satisfied (Rom. 3:25). That's why Paul's little word 'now' is so important. 'Now', in the light of the cross, God cannot and will not condemn those who are in Christ. That would be unjust and it's not going to happen. The judge of the whole earth sees you and says, 'There is now no condemnation!'

In Romans 8, Paul goes on to draw a sharp contrast between living in the 'flesh' or the 'sinful nature' as opposed to living in the 'Spirit'. Not only have we died to sin (Rom. 6), but now the Spirit who raised Jesus from death is alive in us (8:11). The Spirit of resurrection lifts us out of sin so we can live a new life. Paul therefore frames life in the Spirit as an atmosphere or 'realm' (8:9) in which a different set of forces are at work.

I once had the privilege of trying out a flight simulator that is used to train fighter pilots and astronauts. The gravity-defying conditions felt so strange as my body operated in a completely different realm. Laws we assume to be inevitable no longer dominated. In the same way, Paul introduces the Holy Spirit as the one who 'has set you free from the law of sin and death' (8:2).

Paul's use of the word 'law' in Romans is complex. Sometimes it refers to the old covenant made with Israel. On other occasions it may refer to moral standards or commandments. However, in these verses, I believe the term 'law' refers to a basic set of principles that affect all humans, rather like the laws of physics. In other words, imagine sin to be like gravity, dragging us down. In Adam, the 'law of sin and death' held us down in condemnation. However, Paul introduces a new principle, 'the law of the Spirit' (8:2). Rather like an aerodynamic force, the Spirit now lifts us out of the dominion of sin and empowers us to rise up and fulfil God's vision for our lives.

> BECAUSE 'SIN' HAS BEEN CONDEMNED, THE
> NEW LIFE OF THE RESURRECTION, PUT INTO
> OPERATION THROUGH THE SPIRIT, IS NOW
> AT WORK TO SET THE MESSIAH'S PEOPLE
> FREE FROM SIN IN THE PRESENT (8.5–8) AND
> FROM DEATH ITSELF IN THE FUTURE.
> N. T. Wright and M. F. Bird [2]

As a result, the status we were given through justification gradually becomes our lifestyle. Having been declared 'righteous', the Spirit helps us to live a life of righteousness. He brings us into a 'realm' where holy desires and habits are cultivated. He takes things that otherwise felt like a burden – Scripture, prayer, worship, giving, holiness, mission – and transforms them into a source of energy and motivation.

Imagine a hiker carrying a heavy rucksack full of supplies. Even though it's all good stuff, the burden weighs them down. However, when the hiker stops to open the flask and wolf down the sandwiches, what was a burden now becomes energy. In the same way, the Holy Spirit takes spiritual provisions and internalises them so that we can live a new life. Paul sums this up with a remarkable promise: 'the righteous requirement of the law might be fully met in us, who do not live according to the flesh but according to the Spirit' (8:4). This is in direct contrast to the anguished cry of Romans 7 – abject failure becomes joyful obedience, energised by the Spirit.

Therefore, when we are united with Christ and filled with

the Spirit, guilty cycles of sin no longer need to be normal.
We are not condemned to repeat offending. There is hope.
The gospel brings us into a realm where righteousness reigns.
I appreciate this may sound challenging, but I say this for our
good. It's all too easy to resign ourselves to sinful patterns of
behaviour and excuse them: *It's just the way I am. After all,
I'm only human.* But false humility is of no help here. Paul
argues that we have been bought out of slavery to sin by the
blood of Jesus. The Spirit who raised Christ from the dead is
at work in us (8:11), so we don't need to adopt a posture of
resignation. Instead, Paul says, 'Put to death the misdeeds of
the body' (8:13), 'have [your]minds set on what the Spirit
desires' (8:5). Fulfil the 'righteous requirement of the law'
(8:4).

And remember, even when we fail, Romans 8 is what we need
to come back to. Underline key phrases until the ink bleeds
through to the back of your Bible! Let the truth of the gospel
displace every lie from the devil: 'There is now no condemnation for those who are in Christ Jesus'.

Justification > **Adoption** > Glorification
(8:1-11)   **(8:12-17)**   (8:18-30)

High on the summit of Romans, Paul points to another vista of
truth. Having addressed our past, now he considers our status
in the present: 'For those who are led by the Spirit of God are
the children of God' (8:14). Once again, the Spirit is the key. In
fact, after seven chapters of relative silence, the word 'Spirit'
appears seventeen times in quick succession. It is the Holy
Spirit who secures our place in God's household, not as slaves
but as children.

In verse 15, Paul makes this explicit: 'the Spirit you received brought about your adoption to sonship' (8:15). The term 'sonship' is used here because under Roman law, it was a privilege for a male to be adopted into a more prestigious family. Indeed, many Roman rulers were themselves adopted. Julius Caesar passed on his rule to an adopted son, Caesar Augustus. He in turn adopted Tiberius, who was succeeded by two rulers, one of whom was an adopted grandson called Caligula. Under Roman law, if you were adopted into a powerful family your life would change dramatically. All former debts were cancelled and the family name was conferred on you, along with a share of the inheritance equal to that of a natural-born son. Paul sees this as a perfect analogy for the gospel. By nature, God the Father has one eternal Son, Jesus Christ. Yet by grace, the divine family is open to destitute orphans like us. The court-room of acquittal (3:19–25) has become a scene of adoption. Justification brings us into the family of God, which traces all the way back to Abraham (Rom. 4).

This may sound great if you are male, but doesn't 'sonship' play into the hands of patriarchy? Don't we need more gender-inclusive language here? I understand the concern, but if you look carefully, this passage in Romans actually placed a ticking time bomb under ancient prejudices, and the ramifications are still being experienced today. In first-century culture, the head of the home, or *paterfamilias*, would have designated the eldest son to be the main heir of the family estate. By contrast, daughters did not have the same rights or privileges and were more vulnerable as a result. Indeed, unwanted female babies were sometimes 'exposed' or left to die outdoors while male children were adopted into the family.[3] In this patriarchal context, notice what Paul does. He begins with a male term, which more literal translations rightly render 'son'

(v. 15) but then he switches to a more generic Greek word used to refer to 'children' (v. 16), whether male or female. By implication, the titles and privileges, which would normally be reserved for sons, now belong to all God's children. On this occasion, gender-inclusive language would actually obscure the radical nature of the gospel.[4] To imply that a female slave in a filthy attic in the least desirable postcode in Rome is a 'son' of God is theological dynamite. Historian Tom Holland therefore concludes that Christianity was like a cuckoo in the Roman nest.[5] It displaced male patriarchy with an alternative truth – men and women are equally loved and valued by God.

In verse 17, Paul presses the point home: 'Now if we are children, then we are heirs – heirs of God and co-heirs with Christ' (8:17). If an adopted child wanted to know for sure whether their status was truly equal, they might be tempted to look at the family will. Few things are more controversial than the distribution of inheritance among relatives. Sure enough, Paul looks into God's will and sees that we are not just mentioned in passing. We are 'co-heirs with Christ', gifted an equal share of the Father's estate! The only difference is that we inherit upon our own death, not his.

THIS IS THE WONDROUS EXCHANGE MADE BY HIS BOUNDLESS GOODNESS. HAVING BECOME WITH US THE SON OF MAN, JESUS HAS MADE US WITH HIMSELF SONS OF GOD. BEING THUS RECONCILED BY THE RIGHTEOUSNESS OF CHRIST, GOD BECOMES, INSTEAD OF A JUDGE, AN INDULGENT FATHER.

John Calvin, French Reformer in the sixteenth century[6]

By the way, the quote by John Calvin is a favourite of mine. I remember reading it while researching for my master's dissertation. As I understood the beautiful symmetry – he became what we are (Son of Man) so that we might become what he is (sons of God) – I had such an insight into the grace of God that it left me sobbing in the university library. From that day on, my prayer life changed. I no longer imagined myself approaching a stern judge but rather an indulgent father.

In truth, whatever our relationship has been like with our earthly parents, the Spirit introduces us to a heavenly Father who is perfect. So don't project your family history on to this story. You've been adopted into God's family. It's different here.

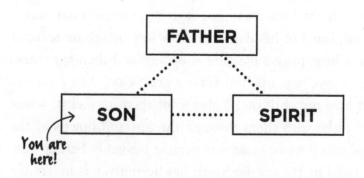

Adoption means we are children of God 'in Christ'

In verses 15 and 16, Paul picks up on how we should speak to God in prayer: 'we cry, "*Abba*, Father." The Spirit himself testifies with our spirit that we are God's children.' He bears witness to the love of God *for us* and causes us to experience the love of God *in us*. *Abba* was an Aramaic term that expressed both profound respect and close intimacy. It was perhaps the equivalent of 'Papa'. It's an intimate term, used by grown-ups and children alike.

In the Middle East, *Abba* is often still the first word children say. On a previous trip to Israel, a boy came running towards us as we emerged through arrivals at Tel Aviv airport. A passenger in front of me then got floored by the boy, who kept shouting, *'Abba! Abba!'* This is the cry the Spirit draws out of us in prayer. Away with polite religion and fancy speeches, this Spirit-inspired cry comes from the heart.

Abba was the term Jesus used to address the Father. Now his intimate approach has become our own. The Father loves us as he loves Jesus, and the Spirit helps us experience this great love. As Paul puts it, 'the Spirit himself testifies with our spirit that we are God's children' (8:16).

To be honest, I've been in a bit of a bad mood today. I think it all traces back to what happened after breakfast. One of my sons left the house without saying goodbye. That may sound trivial, but I'm his dad and every day before he leaves I give him a hug, pray a blessing over him and then say something like, 'I love you, my boy. Have a great day!' As a father I don't just love my children, I also want them to feel it. I want my love to be with them through the ups and downs of the day. How much more must our perfect heavenly Father want this for us? The reason the Spirit has been given is to 'testify' and continually remind us of the Father's love so we can live in the good of it.

Justification > Adoption > **Glorification**
(8:1-11)   (8:12-17)   **(8:18-30)**

Paul's mention of inheritance reminds me of the child inheritance bond that was set up in my name when I was born. When I later became aware of it as a teenager, I felt like I had a whole new reason for living! Then, when I turned twenty-one, I finally got to cash it in. This is how hope works in the New Testament. At the point of our adoption into God's family, we become co-heirs with Christ, whether we realise it or not. We have an inheritance coming our way. It's just a matter of time. In Romans 8, Paul reveals the wonder of what lies in store. It's enough to give us a whole new reason for living. Meanwhile, the Holy Spirit is like a 'deposit' (2 Cor. 1:22). He secures our inheritance until one day, we will be 'old' enough to enjoy it for eternity.

This section of Romans 8 therefore gives a glimpse of our ultimate hope. When times are tough and suffering hits, knowing that a glorious future lies ahead can keep us going. We all engage in mental equations to determine whether present effort and cost is worthwhile. *Shall I keep going to the gym, be part of a church, complete a training course, stay faithful to my spouse?* Too often, short-sighted thinking means we quit early and regret it later. Romans 8 inspires us to take the long view. Our inheritance will be worth every bit of pain and sacrifice. As the Apostle Paul noted elsewhere – and remember, he'd been beaten unconscious, shipwrecked and imprisoned multiple times – 'our light and momentary troubles are achieving for us an eternal glory that far outweighs them all' (2 Cor. 4:17).

By the way, when Paul used the word 'glory', as a Jew he had something different in mind to the Romans. They used the Latin word *gloria* to refer to prowess, victory and splendour – much like our notions of fame and success. However, in the Jewish language of Hebrew, the word for 'glory' (*chabod*) means 'heavy' or 'weighty'. It conveys the idea of a reality that is both aesthetically beautiful and materially substantial. So in the verse above, Paul is claiming that our future state will be more substantial ('outweigh') and more beautiful than anything we have known to date. Bear that in mind as we now consider the theme of glory in Romans 8.

IN LIGHT OF HEAVEN, THE WORST SUFFERING ON EARTH WILL BE SEEN TO BE NO MORE SERIOUS THAN ONE NIGHT IN AN INCONVENIENT HOTEL.
Teresa of Ávila (1515–1582)

So, what is our inheritance according to Romans 8? In short, we look forward to bodily resurrection (8:23), spiritual glorification (8:30) and a renewed material creation (8:21). Sound good? According to verse 19, it is going to be so beautiful, creation itself is waiting with 'eager expectation'. However, what strikes me most is the interrelationship between humans and the natural world. For Paul, they are more intricately connected than David Attenborough or Greta Thunberg would dare to imagine. Think back to Genesis, when God formed the first man from the dust of the ground. In fact, his name (*Adam*) and the word for ground (*adamah*) are almost identical in Hebrew. He could have been called 'Dusty'. No surprise, then, that when Adam and Eve rebelled against God the whole environment fell under a curse (Gen. 3:17). From floods to drought, global warming to plastic waste, according to the Bible, humans are responsible for the plight of the world.

Now follow the logic the other way. If a new humanity should emerge, purged of sin and reflecting God's image, the curse on the environment would be broken and our planet would flourish once again. The arrival of a new Adam (Christ), who redeems a new humanity (Christians), is therefore music to the ears of all creation. The redemption of humanity includes the promise of a renewed creation. Remember, the gospel is not only personal and relational. It is also cosmic good news.

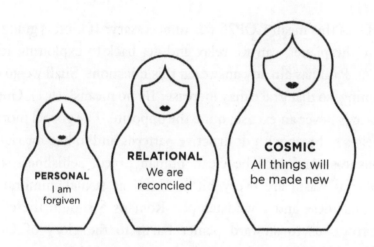

As I write, world leaders are gathering in Glasgow for COP26 to address the challenge of global warming. The situation is so serious that many are speculating whether it is too late to avoid an ecological catastrophe. Romans 8 sympathises with these fears. Human selfishness has dragged the natural environment down into a state of 'bondage to decay' (8:21) or, as the ecologist and Philosopher Aldo Leopold put it, 'a world of wounds'.[7] However, Paul's vision is fundamentally hopeful because, in the end, God's grace will triumph over human sin. After all, that is the essence of the gospel. And it applies not just to souls but also to deserts and daisies and dolphins. With this hope in mind, Paul therefore reinterprets the pain of creation in a more positive way: 'the whole of creation has been groaning *as in the pains of childbirth*' (8:22, italics added). Left in the hands of selfish humans, there's every reason to forecast doom. However, Romans is concerned with God's purpose for planet Earth. This tells a more hopeful story because of the intervening grace of our Lord Jesus Christ. As surely as we humans have 'redemption . . . through the shedding of his blood' (3:24–5), so also 'creation itself will be liberated' (8:21).

Does this mean COP26 was unnecessary? If God is going to save the planet, can we relax and get back to exploiting it? I think Paul has already answered this question: 'Shall we go on sinning, so that grace may increase? By no means!' (6:1). God's grace is never an excuse; quite the opposite. The gospel motivates us to break with destructive patterns and to live for righteousness. And let's be clear, human greed, selfishness and material waste are every bit as sinful as sexual immorality, drunkenness and a wild temper. Romans 8 should therefore motivate us to steward planet Earth to the glory of God. Precisely because we believe the material world has a future, we should be fully invested in the present. Motivated by hope, Christian reformers have taken on terrible evils such as slavery, child poverty and racial inequality. Now one of the great needs of the hour is creation care.

> THE CHALLENGE FOR US EVEN AT THIS MOMENT
> OF CLIMATE COLLAPSE, IS ALWAYS . . . TO
> RE-ENVISION THE BELEAGUERED WORLD WE
> SEE TODAY WITH GOD'S EYES . . . [AND TO]
> INTERPRET CREATION'S PRESENT 'GROANING'
> IN LIGHT OF THE GLORIOUS PURPOSE
> REVEALED BY THE CREATOR IN SCRIPTURE.
> Allen Goddard, A Rocha International[8]

After revealing this global perspective, Paul considers the embodied future that we humans can look forward to: 'Not only so, but we ourselves, who have the first fruits of the Spirit, groan inwardly as we wait eagerly for our adoption to sonship, the redemption of our bodies' (8:23). If you enjoy the starter course at a restaurant, it only whets your appetite for what's to come. Our experience of adoption through the Spirit is merely a foretaste of the main course. As Christ experienced physical resurrection, those who die in Christ will be resurrected like him. Paul therefore refers to 'the redemption of our bodies' (8:23). Our sick, frail, sinful, bodies will one day be metamorphosed in glory. As God's redeemed people, we are being led by the Spirit through many trials and tribulations, just as Israel had to move through the wilderness towards the Promised Land. But one day we shall cross the Jordan river and enter our 'inheritance' – a resurrected body fit for purpose in a restored creation.

So whatever state you're in now, whether you enjoy a good workout in the gym or you struggle to get up from the couch, your best days lie ahead of you. Our bodies will be purged of all sin, sickness, suffering and death and will be eternally renewed by an infusion of the very glory of God. The theological term for all this is *glorification*. Imagine a metal poker thrust into a fiery furnace. Soon the iron glows red as it takes on the likeness of the fire. In the same way, we will be immersed in the very beauty and glory of God and will once again take on his perfect likeness. In the light of this hope, we should be standing on tiptoes. We are on our way from groans to glory.

> FOR THAT FUTURE REDEMPTION WE MUST
> LONG AND WAIT, MAINTAINING ALWAYS
> THE TWO-WORLD, HOMEWARD-TRAVELLING,
> HOPING-FOR-GLORY PERSPECTIVE THAT
> PERVADES THE WHOLE NEW TESTAMENT.
> J. I. Packer[9]

In order to convey how certain this is, in verse 30 Paul dictated one of the most daring sentences in the entire Bible. He outlined four features of God's work in our lives, which are all linked together like a golden chain: 'those [God] predestined, he also called; those he called, he also justified; those he justified, he also glorified'. Notice the first three events have already happened. Glorification is the exception because from our perspective it lies in the future. Nevertheless, Paul says 'glorified'. His deliberate use of the past tense conveys how secure our hope is. From God's perspective, our future is guaranteed because it is grounded in his unfailing purpose and unwavering love.

> CHRISTIANS ARE ABLE TO LOOK BACK
> 'DOWN' THE CHAIN, AND KNOW THAT
> BEFORE CREATION GOD FORE-LOVED THEM,
> AND PREDESTINED THEM TO BE JUSTIFIED.
> AND A CHRISTIAN CAN LOOK ON 'UP' THE
> CHAIN, AND KNOW THAT IN ETERNITY THEY
> WILL KNOW UNIMAGINABLE GLORY.
> Tim Keller[10]

Romans 8 gives a 360-degree panorama of God's great purpose. Looking back, we see that our past no longer determines our future: 'there is no condemnation for those who are in Christ

Jesus'! In the present, the Holy Spirit adopts us into God's family: through him we cry, '*Abba*, Father.' Then, as we look to the far horizon, we stand on tiptoes in 'eager expectation' for the glory that will be revealed. What a view!

REFLECT: Romans 8 sheds the light of hope into the shadows of suffering. What aspect of our future hope are you 'groaning' for and most looking forward to? How does this hope reframe our struggles in this life?

◌⟩◌ Part 2: God is for us

READ: Romans 8:31–39

Today, we live in a culture that has largely ditched the idea of eternity. Instead, the modern assumption is that we need to get rich, get laid and get happy ASAP because this life is all we've got. As the secular acronym puts it, YOLO – *You Only Live Once*. However, people in our society also experience harmful levels of anxiety and stress. Do you think there might be a link? Consider the rise of mental-health issues such as the *Fear of Missing Out* (FOMO). If this life is all there is, it's easy to struggle with long-term commitment: *What if I become trapped and miserable? What if I miss out?*

Romans 8 provides a different way of seeing life. Instead of short-sighted vision that collapses everything into this life, we have the hope of eternal life. Like Moses who stood on Mount Nebo and gazed into the Promised Land, we need to look long and hard at these promises. One day, our resurrected toes will stand on solid ground in a renewed cosmos. There will be no more death, global warming, mourning or pain. In the meantime, hope gives resilience so we can keep going and never give up.

I often read true survival stories with our children, as they highlight important values like resilience, loyalty and courage. But hope is invariably the decisive factor. I recently reread *Man's Search for Meaning*, a remarkable book by Holocaust survivor Victor Frankl. His take-home observation from time spent in Nazi concentration camps was that those who lost hope were the first to die. But those who held on to a greater sense of purpose often lived to tell the tale.

The Christian life does not promise to be easy. As well as

inheriting Christ's estate we 'share in his sufferings' (8:17). At the end of Romans 8, Paul lists seventeen possible calamities (vv. 35–8). His list includes every difficulty we may face. 'Persecution' or unfair treatment, 'famine' or economic crisis, 'powers' or oppressive people, 'sword' or the fear of violence. But in the face of every threat and uncertainty, Paul is convinced that nothing can 'separate us from the love of God'. So he roars hope over every challenge: 'we are more than conquerors through him who loved us' (8:37).

In the final section of Romans 8, Paul delivers a flurry of now famous verses. They include rhetorical questions that are designed to help us pause and reflect on the implications of all that we have seen in this chapter:

> What, then, shall we say in response to these things? If God is for us, who can be against us? He who did not spare his own Son, but gave him up for us all – how will he not also, along with him, graciously give us all things?
>
> *Romans 8:31–2*

Paul's logic here is impeccable. In fact, this whole section is logic on fire! If God has done the hard thing – given his Son for us – he's not going to shy away from the easy thing. We can be confident that our Father in heaven will give us everything we need to get the job done. As Paul put it in one of his other letters, 'He who began a good work in you will carry it on to completion' (Phil. 1:6). Paul's confidence is rooted in the cross of Christ, where God demonstrated his love for us. Nothing can hold him back now. God is a completer-finisher. He will bring to perfection every person who trusts in him.

This leads to another question which contains its own answer: 'If God is for us, who can be against us?' Or we might say, 'Who would dare be against us if God is with us?' If Almighty God is by our side, what can take away our hope or rob us of our peace? Whatever challenges we may face, our situation is not our identity. Even when we are in great danger, we are always in Christ, and that makes us secure. 'Persecution' 'danger', 'sword' – these are just circumstances. But my life is hidden in Christ. I am who he says I am. Nothing compares to the promise I have in Jesus. No threat is greater than the power of the Spirit. Life is not defined by our problems or failings because God is *for* us.

I recall one of my earliest mountain climbs with my father. I may have been six years old. As we got up onto the summit ridge, the wind became strong and I was afraid it would blow me off the cliff. I lost all awareness of the view and stumbled to the ground in fear. My father realised what was happening but was not going to let this challenge turn us back. So he took the dog's lead and tied me to himself. Now, when you are six, your dad is huge! Suddenly, the fear dissipated, my head lifted and soon we were enjoying sandwiches on the summit. Romans 8 reminds us that we are tied to our heavenly Father by an unbreakable chain – nothing can separate us from his love. So there is no need to turn back in fear. We are more than conquerors!

> PAUL IS SAYING: ARE YOU WORRIED (V 32)?
> YOU AREN'T THINKING! ARE YOU FEELING
> GUILTY (V 33)? YOU AREN'T THINKING!
> DO YOU FEAR THE FUTURE (V 35)? YOU
> AREN'T THINKING! SEE THE LOGIC OF GOD'S
> GRACE. THESE AREN'T DRY DOCTRINES;
> THEY ARE LIFE ITSELF. WE ARE MORE THAN
> CONQUERORS THROUGH HIM WHO LOVES US!
> Martyn Lloyd-Jones[11]

In another famous verse, Paul gives more detail on how God oversees our hope: 'we know that in all things God works for the good of those who love him, who have been called according to his purpose' (8:28). Notice the daring use of the word 'all'. It includes evil people, sinful choices, tragic accidents and inexplicable suffering. Supremely, the cross demonstrated that God can take the very worst event in history and turn it into a triumph. He can do the same in our lives too. We may not always see how this works from our side. But in the light of the end, from the perspective of eternity, God promises to work all things for good. So remember that next time the bottom falls out of life and things feel hopeless. God works for our good in spite of the bad. In the end, we will be more than conquerors.

At the end of this chapter, having surveyed a stunning 360-degree panorama of truth, we need time to let it all sink in. It's not enough simply to read it. We need to wear it like lenses through which we see all of life. I find if I memorise key phrases and regularly remind myself of them, fear is displaced by truth. Then hope becomes the soundtrack of my soul.

REFLECT: Personalise these phrases from Romans 8 with your name and try speaking them out loud. Which do you find most difficult to believe? Ask God to bring it home for you.

There is now no condemnation for _____ who is in Christ Jesus (v. 1).
The Spirit of him who raised Jesus from the dead is living in _____ (v. 11).
In all things God works for the good of _____ who loves him and is called according to his purpose (v. 28).
If God is for _____, who can be against _____ (v. 31)?

[Nothing] will be able to separate _____ from the love of God (v. 39).

We wait eagerly for our adoption to sonship, the redemption of our bodies. For in this hope we were saved.

Romans 8:23–4

7

The cloud of mystery

Romans 9:1—11:36

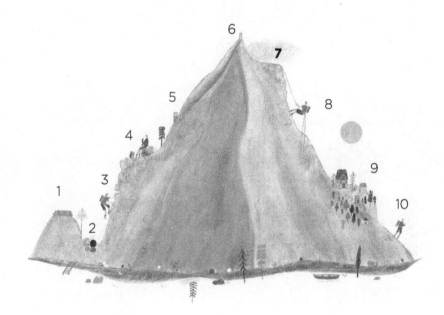

I hope you enjoyed the view from the summit of Romans 8. We will need the inspiration for the next stage of our adventure. The truth is, if you climb mountains there will be times when you become engulfed in thick mist while crossing rough terrain. The summit plateau of Ben Nevis, the highest mountain in Britain, is covered in cloud on average three hundred days of the year! So, if you happen to get a view on the top, don't be surprised if the mist then closes in. These are testing times when you have to dig deep, trust the compass and hope the clouds part soon.

For many of us, Paul's argument in Romans 9—11 will feel like the mist closing in. These chapters form the most dense and intricate argument anywhere in Paul's letters. The overarching theme is the sovereignty of God, including why he chooses certain people to fulfil his purpose. In particular, this section reveals God's sovereign plan for Israel as his chosen people, stretching back to Abraham and forward into the future. Imagine Romans 9—11 as a fresh retelling of Israel's story but now with Jesus as its climax – 'Christ is the culmination of the law' (10:4). Paul was himself a Jew. So he was eager to demonstrate that God had not given up on his chosen people, even if they seemed to be rejecting their own Messiah. As we shall see, Paul concludes this whole section with a sensational promise: 'all Israel will be saved' (11:26).

While that headline sounds encouraging, Romans 9—11 raises some knotty questions: *Is there a special, elect group of people who are saved no matter what? Are other people simply damned whatever they do? Does God's covenant with Israel justify their ongoing conflict in the Middle East?* Welcome to the cloud of mystery. On the one hand, these issues should not become divisive. However, the fact that Paul devotes one-fifth of the letter to addressing them shows how important they are to his overall argument.

Don't think of Romans 9—11 as an anticlimax. We are still high up on the mountain. In Romans 12 we will begin our descent, 'in view of God's mercy' (12:1). But first Paul must address concerns that would have surfaced in the minds of Phoebe's audience in Rome. As they took in the panoramic view of Romans 8, perhaps they began to wonder: *Hang on a minute. What happened to Israel? We Gentiles made it to the summit, but have the chosen people failed to reach the climax of their own story?* Understandably, they would have assumed that when the Messiah came the Jewish nation would be the first to join his movement. But the opposite seemed to be happening as the Jewish people not only rejected Christ but also sought to eradicate his followers.

Yet Paul is clear that Israel's past will not have the final word. In the future, God will bring about a widespread revival among his chosen people. So the clouds do part by the end of Romans 11 and Paul concludes with a magnificent outburst of praise:

Oh, the depth of the riches of the wisdom and knowledge of
    God!
How unsearchable his judgments,
and his paths beyond tracing out!
'Who has known the mind of the Lord?
Or who has been his counsellor?'
'Who has ever given to God,
that God should repay them?'
For from him and through him and for him are all things.
To him be the glory forever! Amen.

Romans 11:33–6

This outburst captures an important tension that we must learn to live with. On the one hand, God is sovereign so we will never fully understand his 'unsearchable' ways. His paths are 'beyond tracing out' (v. 33). So there are mysteries in life that cannot be neatly resolved. Perhaps you have experienced this in a personal way – inexplicable loss, unanswered prayers, seemingly unfulfilled promises. Romans 9—11 is a reminder that being a Christian does not mean we have all the answers. Rather, we have somewhere to go with our questions – a loving heavenly Father whom we can trust even when life doesn't make sense.

The first time I climbed Ben Nevis, the summit was covered in cloud and thick snow. As we began our descent, I headed straight down the slope, until I heard my father yell, 'Stop!' Unbeknown to me, a deep gulley cuts into the summit plateau. In winter, you could walk through a hidden cornice of snow and fall to your death. So my father insisted that we take the long way round.

Sometimes in life we can't see the dangers that lie beneath the surface, nor can we appreciate all that God knows. So we have to trust our heavenly Father when the clouds come down. Perhaps God is taking you the long way round for a reason?

However, even though God is sovereign we still have a part to play. Alongside certain mysteries, God has clearly revealed the core truths of the gospel and called us to take action in the light of them. Romans 9—11 therefore shows us how to hold both truths in tension: to live with revelation and mystery while trusting in the sovereignty of God and taking our responsibilities seriously. A verse in the Old Testament sums it up well: 'The secret things belong to the LORD our God, but the things revealed belong to us and to our children for ever' (Deut. 29:29).

Part 1: God is sovereign

In this section we consider God's election of Israel in the past (Rom. 9) and God's promise to redeem Israel in the future (Rom. 11).

○─○ Part 2: We have a part to play

Here we focus on Romans 10 where Paul clarifies the role that we must play, confessing that 'Jesus is Lord' and sharing the gospel with all people.

> Oh, the depth of the riches of the wisdom and knowledge of God! How unsearchable his judgments, and his paths beyond tracing out!
>
> *Romans 11:33*

Part 1: God is sovereign

READ: Romans 9:1–33; 11:1–36

Several years before Phoebe delivered Paul's letter to Rome, Emperor Claudius banished all Jews from living in the city. He accused them of causing 'disturbances', framed them as troublemakers and forced them to leave their homes and live in exile elsewhere. Anti-Jewish politics are therefore a crucial part of the backstory to Paul's letter. Gentile believers would have got used to being the only Christians in town and no doubt began to assume they could sever the Jewish roots of their faith. However, after Claudius' death in AD 54, some Jewish Christians began to return to Rome. Can you imagine the atmosphere that greeted them? An air of mistrust and suspicion, even within the Christian community.

Sadly, antisemitism has been a problem ever since. In the twentieth century, Nazi soldiers rounded up the Jewish population of Rome and put them on trains to death camps such as Auschwitz. At times, the Christian church has been guilty of colluding with the oppressors.[1] Today, antisemitism seems to be on the rise again in Europe. As I write this, there is footage on the national news of young men spitting at Jewish teenagers in London. Beneath the hatred lurks a dangerous ideology that needs to be exposed. Romans 9—11 provides an opportunity to reflect on how we think and talk about Jewish people. Instead of suspicion or mistrust, Paul's opening paragraph captures God's heart:

I have great sorrow and unceasing anguish in my heart. For I could wish that I myself were cursed [literally *anathema*] and cut off from Christ for the sake of my people, those of my own

race, the people of Israel . . . Theirs are the patriarchs, and
from them is traced the human ancestry of the Messiah, who is
God over all, forever praised! Amen.

Romans 9:2–5

Paul's language is deliberately arresting. He wants those listening
to feel his pain. Eugene Peterson captured it well in his paraphrase:
'If there were any way I could be cursed by the Messiah so they
could be blessed by him, I'd do it in a minute' (9:2, MSG).

Perhaps you identify strongly with a people group or tribe
and it hurts to see them spiritually lost? Paul's passion for 'my
people' reminds us that even though we are all one in Christ,
national identity still matters. If you are Jewish, it's right to feel
passionate about Israel; if you are Welsh, about Wales, and so
on. The real challenge is how we balance deep anguish for those
we love with an even deeper trust in the sovereignty of God.
That's what Paul is grappling with in Romans 9—11.

God's election of Israel in the past

Paul's first response is to delve back into Israel's past and trace
out a hidden plotline of election:

> It is not as though God's word had failed. For not all who are
> descended from Israel are Israel. Nor because they are his
> descendants are they all Abraham's children. On the contrary,
> 'It is through Isaac that your offspring will be reckoned.' In
> other words, it is not the children by physical descent who are
> God's children, but it is the children of the promise who are
> regarded as Abraham's offspring.
>
> *Romans 9:6–8*

Paul's argument makes a vital distinction between Jewish *ethnicity* that is visible and divine *election* that is unseen. As Paul applies this to Israel's family tree, it becomes clear that DNA is not the decisive factor in identifying the true people of God. Some who were physically descended from Abraham were not part of the chosen people. After all, his descendants included not only Isaac but also Ishmael, as well as other sons mentioned in Genesis 25. However, it is clear that only Isaac was the promised child. Equally, Isaac's twin boys, Esau and Jacob, were born of the same parents on the same day. Yet even before they emerged from Rebekah's womb, God had predetermined that Jacob would be the chosen one, not Esau (Gen. 25:23). This subverted an ancient custom whereby the firstborn inherited a greater blessing. Instead, another mysterious plotline was unfolding:

> In order that God's purpose in election might stand: not by works but by him who calls – [Rebekah] was told, 'The older will serve the younger.' Just as it is written: 'Jacob I loved, but Esau I hated.'
>
> *Romans 9:11–13*

This last phrase is a Jewish idiom that uses hyperbole to make a point. God didn't literally 'hate' Esau any more than Jesus meant that we should 'hate' our father and mother (Luke 14:26). But if you were Esau, it might have felt this way as you witnessed your younger brother clearly experiencing preferential treatment. In the Genesis narrative, a spotlight seems to follow Jacob wherever he went. On one occasion he was wrestled to the ground, blessed and renamed 'Israel' by the angel of the LORD (Gen. 32). All this in spite of the fact that Jacob was a deceptive, insecure and proud man. Paul's point is that only a decision by God himself could account for the role Jacob was given.

Understandably, we might consider someone a Jew according to their ethnicity or *nature*. But from God's perspective, the chosen people have always been elected by *grace*. Paul's sketch of Israel's history in Romans 9 shows that God always acts on this basis. His decisions are not based on things we can observe such as human merit or status.

By this point, I imagine your blood is beginning to boil. Here we are, trying to develop fairer societies based on equal opportunities. Meanwhile, God is undermining the whole thing with random acts of favouritism. How is divine election fair? Doesn't it create a Christian equivalent of the caste system where some are born elites and others are 'untouchable' toilet cleaners? In Romans 9, Paul himself gives voice to these questions, showing that it is an understandable response: 'What then shall we say? Is God unjust?' (9:14). While we cannot unravel the knot of God's sovereignty, a couple of qualifiers do help to reframe this passage.

First, we need to ask what 'election' means in the Bible. Theologians who study this question disagree at this point. Those referred to as 'Calvinist', named after the sixteenth-century Protestant Reformer John Calvin, argue that God's election is irrespective of human action. God simply chooses some sinners but passes over others. There is no rhyme or reason. It is sheer mystery. On the other hand, 'Arminians' named after another Protestant theologian, Jacob Arminius, argue that God's foreknowledge enables him to see in advance how someone will respond to the gospel. Divine election is therefore in part a response to human action.

Despite considering these debates for years as part of my PhD research, I am still unsure which way to jump. These are truths that must be held in tension. Billy Graham summed up the paradox well. At the entrance to the gates of heaven is a sign saying, 'Come, whosoever will believe.' Then on the inside of the gates is a sign saying, 'Chosen before the foundation of the world.'[2] This mystery reminds us that we need to stay humble and not presume we can solve every problem.

That said, when it comes to Romans 9, it seems to me that Paul's argument is less about *election to salvation* and more about *election to service*. Let me explain. In political discourse today, 'election' means being chosen for a particular task or office. The Greek word *eklektos*, from which we get 'elect', can also be used this way. So, Romans 9 is not necessarily about where Jacob and Esau will spend eternity. Rather, Paul is seeking to explain how God chose or elected Israel to fulfil a special role in world history. I think Romans 8 addresses the issue of eternal salvation (8:29–30). However, Romans 9 focuses on Israel's shared calling or vocation as a nation. That's why Paul prays that Israel 'may be saved' in Romans 10:1, because their 'election' was not about salvation. Rather, in this context, election is the means by which God accomplishes his purposes.[3] The difference is crucial. After all, in the New Testament Jesus chose twelve men to become unique Apostles within his movement. The fact that one of them, Judas, fell from grace shows that *election to service* does not guarantee *election to salvation*. They are distinct issues that need to be handled differently.

THE ENTIRE NARRATIVE OF ROMANS 9—11 IS
NOT ABOUT WHO GETS SAVED IN THE DEEPLY
PERSONAL SENSE BUT ABOUT WHO THE
GOSPEL AGENTS ARE IN GOD'S REDEMPTIVE
PLANS. IT'S ABOUT WHERE WE ARE IN THE
PLAN OF GOD FOR COSMIC REDEMPTION.

Scot McKnight[4]

Of course, this in no way diminishes God's sovereignty. He chose Jacob for a particular calling without any moral basis for the decision. This is what theologians refer to as 'unconditional election'. The reason lies entirely in God and is unrelated to human worth. If we apply this principle today, it helps avoid feelings of inadequacy or superiority. If God has raised you up to serve within a particular ministry or given you special notoriety, do not misinterpret this as something you deserve. Jacob was no better than Esau. Instead, it is a gift to be stewarded to the glory of God.

Equally, where someone else is flourishing and succeeding, we need not become jealous or think of them as rivals. At times I've struggled with this. But the sovereignty of God has helped me to stop looking sideways, comparing myself to others. Instead, I try to remind myself, 'Stay in your lane and run the race marked out for you.' We will enjoy life so much more if we embrace the part we've been chosen to play. Let's not miss God's purpose for our lives because we are distracted by his purpose for someone else.

The second qualifier is that Romans 9 is one of several places in Scripture where we are reminded that we do not line manage God and he does not owe us an explanation. This can be a hard truth for modern ears to hear. Western Christianity can be guilty of domesticating God. We assume he exists to answer our questions and help us fulfil our dreams, much like a divine therapist. Equally, in an age that prizes rational, scientific explanations, our tolerance for mystery is limited. In this context, the second half of Romans 9 can be even more challenging than the first:

> One of you will say to me: 'Then why does God still blame us? For who is able to resist his will?' But who are you, a human being, to talk back to God? 'Shall what is formed say to the one who formed it, "Why did you make me like this?"' Does not the potter have the right to make out of the same lump of clay some pottery for special purposes and some for common use?
>
> *Romans 9:19–21*

Perhaps these verses feel uncomfortable? After all, who does God think he is, refusing to answer our questions? The risk of responding like this is that we swap the living God for a 'nicer', more manageable deity that is a figment of our imagination. When trouble comes and help is needed, that's not much use. It may feel humbling, but there is something deeply reassuring about the overwhelming majesty of God. Precisely because God is great and does not report to us, he is able to take care of us. The last thing we fragile humans need is a god who is just as confused as we are. Instead, when we allow God to be God and cultivate a healthy sense of awe and reverence, the very thing we thought was a problem proves to be a source of peace.

THERE IS NO ATTRIBUTE OF GOD MORE
COMFORTING TO HIS CHILDREN THAN THE
DOCTRINE OF DIVINE SOVEREIGNTY . . .
WHEN YOU GO THROUGH A TRIAL, THE
SOVEREIGNTY OF GOD IS THE PILLOW
UPON WHICH YOU LAY YOUR HEAD.

C. H. Spurgeon[5]

God's purpose for Israel in the future

Having established God's election in the past (Rom. 9), Paul
considers God's purpose for Israel in the future (Rom. 11). It's
worth noting that the very existence of Israel as a distinct
people group today is nothing short of a miracle. I was recently
interviewed with historian Tom Holland on the *Unbelievable?*
show, hosted by Justin Brierley. During our conversation, Tom
argued that within the ancient world Israel had the unique ability to preserve their ethnic and religious identity despite being
repeatedly overrun by larger empires.[6] Today, no one has a
Canaanite, Hittite or Amorite passport. However, despite being
overrun by the Babylonians (sixth century BC), the Romans
(first century) and the Third Reich (twentieth century), the
Jewish people are still standing, even after those empires are
long gone.[7] Why? I believe the answer lies in the sovereignty of
God. He has preserved Israel because they were originally his
covenant people and he still has a special purpose for them.

We shouldn't therefore assume that the Christian church has
simply swallowed up Israel. This idea is known as 'replacement
theology', or supersessionism, and for me, it doesn't do justice
to the promises in Romans 11. Paul is clear that there is still a
special purpose for Israel that is not true of other nations or
people groups.

So what end-time calling still awaits the descendants of Abraham, Isaac and Jacob? Contrary to the teaching of some Christian Zionists, I don't believe Romans 11 addresses geopolitical events, nor does it predict the establishment of the State of Israel in 1947. God's future promises to Israel should not be confused with occupying territory in the Middle East, and they certainly don't justify ongoing hostilities between Israelis and Palestinians.[8] God's ultimate purpose is far more significant than one patch of real estate. In Romans 4:13 the promise to Abraham was that his offspring would become 'heirs of the world'. What a breathtaking promise for a small nomadic family! The Promised Land of Canaan was therefore symbolic, pointing forward to the end time renewal of all creation.

In Romans 11, Paul therefore draws on a complex horticultural metaphor involving an olive tree to reimagine Israel's future. Under rare circumstances, it may be possible to reinvigorate a dormant olive tree by grafting into it a new shoot.[9] Paul applies the metaphor specifically to 'you Gentiles' (11:13). The Christian church has emerged from Jewish roots, rather like 'a wild olive shoot' (v. 17) stemming from an old olive tree. So it is completely inappropriate for a Christian to disrespect the source from which they have come. Ultimately, as a Gentile Christian, I read Jewish Scriptures and worship an olive-skinned Messiah!

In the future, God's ultimate purpose is to use this Gentile ingrafting to stimulate new growth in Israel. Though Israel was 'broken off' (11:20) as a result of rejecting their Messiah, one day God will graft them back in (11:24). Jew and Gentile will finally bear fruit together to the glory of God! *The Message* helpfully summarises Paul's teaching in this complex section:

There was a time not so long ago when you [Gentiles] were on the outs with God. But then the Jews slammed the door on him and things opened up for you. Now *they* are on the outs. But with the door held wide open for you, they have a way back in . . . God makes sure that we all experience what it means to be outside so that he can personally open the door and welcome us back in!

Romans 11:30–2 (MSG)

The vision Paul reveals through this metaphor is quite breathtaking. God has roles worked out for Jew and Gentile, which will result in large-scale blessing for both. In the Old Testament, God elected Israel to be his chosen people, and this made Gentile nations jealous.[10] In the New Testament, all Gentiles can now be welcomed into the family of God. Paul anticipates a day when this will make Israel jealous, resulting in a revival among Jewish people. In the end, 'all Israel will be saved' (11:26).

Paul's headline over Romans 9—11 is therefore quite simple: *Just because Israel seems to have rejected God, do not think God has rejected Israel.* In the end, we can expect many Jews to believe in Jesus Christ. There are some encouraging signs of this happening today.[11] However, we should also remember that in Romans 9 Paul redefined Israel according to election, not ethnicity. We should not assume these end-time promises in Romans 11 refer to every ethnic Jew but rather to God's covenant people 'Israel' as a whole. There will not be two salvation tracks – faith in Christ for Gentiles and a DNA test for Jews.[12] As Romans 1—4 established, Jew and Gentile are united through the Gospel. 'There is no difference . . . for *all* have sinned . . . and *all* are justified freely by his grace' (Rom. 3:22–4, italics added).

I'm sure this leaves you with more questions than answers. However, Paul deliberately finishes this section with a beautiful hymn of worship. It's as if he knows this is as far as we can go in understanding God's sovereign purpose. We must trust God with mysteries beyond our understanding. As Augustine famously noted, if you can understand it, it's probably not God![13] Mystery reassures us that our faith is rooted in something transcendent, beyond our comprehension. I wonder whether Paul had Isaiah 55 in mind as he concluded Romans 11:

> 'For my thoughts are not your thoughts,
> neither are your ways my ways,'
> declares the LORD.
> 'As the heavens are higher than the earth,
> so are my ways higher than your ways
> and my thoughts than your thoughts.'
>
> *Isaiah 55:8–9*

This God can be trusted in the face of life's unanswered questions. After all, when we experience disappointments and tragedies, what we need is not more answers. When has that ever been enough? Instead, we need to rest our head on the pillow of God's sovereignty, knowing that he has promised to work all things together for good. We need to know deep in our souls that the God who rules over the nations (Rom. 9—11) is our '*Abba, Father*' (Rom. 8:15). How about that?

REFLECT: Take a moment to reflect on the verses below. Perhaps kneel as you do this. Surrender to God's purpose and enjoy a moment of childlike wonder.

OH, THE DEPTH OF THE RICHES OF THE
WISDOM AND KNOWLEDGE OF GOD!
HOW UNSEARCHABLE HIS JUDGMENTS,
AND HIS PATHS BEYOND TRACING OUT!
'WHO HAS KNOWN THE MIND OF THE LORD?
OR WHO HAS BEEN HIS COUNSELLOR?'
'WHO HAS EVER GIVEN TO GOD,
THAT GOD SHOULD REPAY THEM?'
FOR FROM HIM AND THROUGH HIM
AND FOR HIM ARE ALL THINGS.
TO HIM BE THE GLORY FOR EVER! AMEN.

Romans 11:33–6

○○ Part 2: We have a part to play

READ: Romans 10:1–21

Have you ever pondered the paradox of light? Elementary physics lessons explain that it sometimes behaves as particles and
other times as waves. One day we might understand this apparent contradiction. In the meantime, these two observable facts sit
alongside each other as a paradox. So it is with God's sovereignty
and our responsibility. The Bible does not categorise events in an
exclusive manner – *this was a God event* or *this was a human event*.
Instead, both are held together: God is in control and yet human
beings are responsible for their actions. The sovereignty of God
is therefore a great comfort when life is tough, but it should never
become an excuse for failing to play our part. Indeed, those who
believe God is sovereign will be more motivated to pray, serve,
give and evangelise, knowing their actions are contributing to the
fulfilment of a larger purpose.

Having *looked into* the mists of God's sovereignty, the clouds
now part and we are able to *look through* and consider the part
we must play. Sandwiched between discussions of Israel's past
election (Rom. 9) and future hope (Rom. 11), is Romans 10,
which emphasises the need for human action. After some deep
theology, it's time to get practical. According to Paul, we must
take responsibility by *confessing* that Jesus is Lord and *communicating* the gospel to all.

Confess that Jesus is Lord: Romans 10:9–13

Since this chapter has involved wrestling with paradoxes, let's
introduce another: *the gospel is radically inclusive and exclusive
at the same time*. In Romans 10, Paul develops a deliberate

contrast between the old covenant and the gospel. He quotes from Leviticus, which teaches that Torah obedience is the key to blessing: 'The person who does these things will live by them' (10:5). However, now a fully obedient Jew has fulfilled the Torah and opened up a new way of blessing, equally available to Jew and Gentile: 'Christ is the culmination of the law so that there may be righteousness for everyone who believes' (10:4). So faith is now the only requirement for joining the covenant people of God. The gospel is therefore radically *inclusive*. God saves Gentiles as Gentiles and Jews as Jews. There is no ethnic bias or racial discrimination. Instead, the message of Jesus is just as native in Johannesburg as in Jerusalem, in Beijing as in Bethlehem. Paul goes on to say, 'For there is no difference between Jew and Gentile – the same Lord is Lord of all and richly blesses all who call on him' (10:12).

Equally, there are no first- and second-class citizens in God's kingdom. The simple truth that '*everyone* who calls on the name of the Lord will be saved' (10:13, italics added) democratised the gospel in a context dominated by social hierarchies and wealth. In Roman culture, you could buy your way into a privileged position. For example, if as a Roman citizen you owned at least four hundred thousand sesterces (approximately £100,000 today), you could become an 'equestrian' or member of the upper class. Or if you were a generous benefactor who owned more than a million sesterces, you could acquire a seat in the famous senate.

Recent scandals in politics show that we are just as culpable of cash for honours or donations for influence. However, the gospel pulls the rug from under elitist hierarchies. You cannot buy salvation. Before God, the rich are as spiritually bankrupt as the poor and those excluded on the margins are just as welcome as those with luxurious villas. In societies marred by inequality and injustice, this message has the power to humble the elite and lift up the downtrodden.

However, Paul goes on to define faith in an exclusive way. It is not enough merely to be 'spiritual' or to vaguely believe in 'God'. The true God has given us his calling card so we can reach out to him by name:

> If you declare with your mouth, 'Jesus is Lord,' and believe in your heart that God raised him from the dead, you will be saved. For it is with your heart that you believe and are justified, and it is with your mouth that you profess your faith and are saved . . . for, 'Everyone who calls on the name of the Lord will be saved.'
>
> *Romans 10:9–10, 13*

The personal name of God was revealed to Moses at the burning bush in Exodus 3. It was so sacred that no Jew would dare to pronounce it when reading the Scriptures out loud. Instead, they replaced the Hebrew four-letter word of God's name (YHWH) with another word: 'LORD'. That's why it appears in small capitals throughout the Old Testament. Imagine the word like a veil covering over something sacred. However, in the New Testament, Jesus Christ has lifted the veil and revealed God personally. That's why Paul considers an Old Testament prophecy about Israel's God (Yahweh or Jehovah) to be fulfilled by Jesus: 'Everyone who calls on the name of the LORD will be saved' (Joel 2:32, quoted in Rom. 10:13, italics added).

The implications of this are enormous. I remember speaking to a Jewish man on a flight to America. When I shared that I was a Christian, his friendly demeanour changed. When I asked what troubled him, he replied, 'You Christians say that Jesus is Lord!' He understood the ramifications of this ancient Christian creed. Jesus bears the name and reveals the nature of the one true God.

In Romans 10, Paul highlights the importance of confessing truth with our mouths. This probably alludes to an early Christian practice whereby a new believer would make a public confession before being baptised in water and welcomed into the church. In first-century Rome, this was a radical thing to do. The emperor considered himself to be 'Lord' or *Kyrios* in Greek. This title was etched on sculptures and stamped on coins, as part of a propaganda machine across the Empire – rather like modern billboards and advertising today.[14] The claim that 'Jesus is Lord' was therefore in direct conflict with political powers. No wonder early Christians like Paul spent considerable time in Roman prisons.

Still today, this exclusive claim is a radical statement to make. It involves standing out from the crowd and declaring in the face of every political, religious or philosophical alternative, 'Jesus is Lord!'

> WHAT THEN, ACCORDING TO THIS SECTION, IS
> NECESSARY TO SALVATION? . . . CALLING ON THE
> NAME OF THE LORD, COMBINING FAITH IN THE
> HEART AND CONFESSION WITH THE MOUTH.
> John Stott[15]

Throughout my teenage years, I lived in fear and hid my faith from others. I wanted to be popular and accepted. Looking back, it was an exhausting way to live. However, I then began to study Romans, with the help of a commentary by John Stott. When I came to this passage in Romans 10, it deeply challenged me. I had believed in my heart but not confessed with my mouth. This brought me to a crossroads.

A few months later, I stood at the front of church, declared, 'Jesus is Lord,' and got baptised to show it. That day was a significant turning point. The hold of fear was broken and I grew in spiritual confidence. Before long, I became more open about my faith. Some of my friends thought I had only just become a Christian as it was the first they'd heard of it! Have you gone public and declared your allegiance to Jesus Christ? Perhaps Romans 10 is stirring you to action?

Communicate the gospel: Romans 10:14–15

If the gospel is radically inclusive (*open to everyone*) and also exclusive (*only through Christ*), what about those who have never heard? Paul doesn't directly answer this question. It is one of the 'secret things' (Deut. 29:29) that belongs to God. In his sovereignty, God will fulfil the promise that everyone who calls on the name of the Lord will be saved. However, what is clear is that we have a part to play. It is now our responsibility to ensure that the message of Jesus is clearly and lovingly communicated.

> How can they believe in the one of whom they have not heard? And how can they hear without someone preaching to them? And how can anyone preach unless they are sent? As it is written: 'How beautiful are the feet of those who bring good news!'
>
> *Romans 10:14–15*

The word translated 'preach' refers to the role of a herald. In the ancient world, before mass communications, a herald was a news-bearer. They would travel to cities, announcing major events in the marketplace and city streets. If you've seen the film *News of the World*, starring Tom Hanks, it conveys the importance of this role for those living in remote communities. A major event may have occurred, such as a military victory or the election of a new ruler. But until the herald arrives, they don't know about it. Paul draws on this metaphor to describe the second responsibility we have as Christians. A major world event has occurred in the arrival of Jesus Christ. His death and resurrection have won the decisive victory for all humanity. However, people will not know about this unless someone communicates with them. So we are called as heralds to leave our comfort zone and go out of our way to share the good news. This is not about sermons on a Sunday but sharing hope with our friends and neighbours.

Paul rounds this section off with an emotive quote from the prophet Isaiah: 'How beautiful are the feet of those who bring good news!' (10:15). Imagine a herald who has run over the mountains and crossed rugged terrain in order to deliver a message of good news. In Israel's case at the time of the prophet Isaiah, it was the announcement that the shame of exile was over. Imagine the state of the messenger's feet by the time they arrived. Bruised, cut, bloodied. The herald has run himself into the ground. When the recipients realise the risks taken to convey the news, they exclaim: *What beautiful feet!*

Herein lies the final paradox of this chapter. If we want to live a meaningful, beautiful life, we must sacrifice ourselves for the cause of Christ. Spiritually speaking, our feet must not be manicured or wrapped in cotton wool. Personally, I find this such a challenge given how comfortable we can be as Christians in the West. I think of friends in a North African country, where it is illegal to be a Christian. By day they run a newspaper printing business, but by night they secretly print Bibles as there is a growing demand in spite of the risks. As the machines clunk away, they hold their breath, praying they won't be detected. But fear doesn't stop their beautiful feet from sharing the truth under the radar of an oppressive state. Romans 10 calls us also to live outside our comfort zone and to communicate the gospel with kindness and courage.

During the 1970s, the Khmer Rouge was a brutal regime that caused terrible bloodshed in Cambodia. Many fled over the border to refugee camps in Thailand. Among them were two friends, aged eleven and thirteen. In the camp they met a Christian missionary called Don Cormack who shared the message of Jesus. Once they experienced the power of the gospel in their own lives, these two boys decided they must take the message back to their own village. So, despite the dangers, they set off to cross the mountains back to Cambodia.

Many months later, Don Cormack saw the older boy returning down the trail. He was pushing a wheelbarrow with two feet poking out the end. It was his friend, who had died of illness after sharing the gospel with his village. As Don helped bury the boy beside the trail, Romans 10:15 came to mind: 'How beautiful are the feet of those who bring good news!'

Finally, we've made it through the cloud of mystery and out the other side. I honestly think Romans 9—11 is the most challenging and rewarding section of the whole letter. From here, it's downhill all the way. But first, let's take stock of what we've learned. One of the things I've noticed about mountain mist is that when you finally emerge into clear air, your vision seems sharper than ever. After a prolonged time in the grey haze, the landscape appears more vibrant and colourful. In the light of God's sovereignty, the part we have to play now comes into sharper focus. We must confess that Jesus is Lord and communicate the gospel to those who have not heard. What might that look like for you?

REFLECT: What would it mean to have 'beautiful feet', going out of your way to share God's love? Write down some specific people and pray for open doors, open hearts and the courage to open your mouth.

_____   _____   _____

Oh, the depth of the riches of the wisdom and knowledge of God! How unsearchable his judgments, and his paths beyond tracing out!

Romans 11:33

8

The descent of devotion

Romans 12:1-21

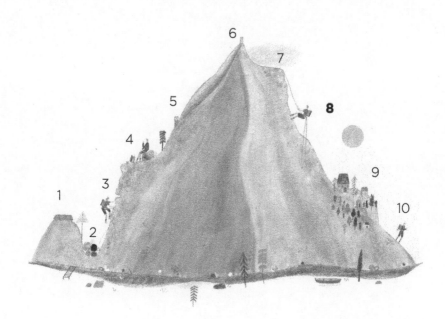

One of my favourite adventures was a winter climb in Scotland. We got up while it was still dark, filled up on porridge and set off into a blanket of freezing fog. The first few hours were exhausting. We ascended a gulley on the north face that was frozen hard and became progressively steeper. With nerves jittering and muscles shaking, our heads eventually popped over the ridge line. I can still remember the feeling of the sun hitting my face as we came over the horizon and stood on level ground. Now, high above the clouds, the view was breathtaking.

THEREFORE, IN VIEW OF GOD'S MERCY . . .
Romans 12:1

It may have felt like hard work to take on the mighty letter to the Romans. We have negotiated some of the most challenging terrain in the Bible. But what a view we now have of God's great purpose, stretching back to the dawn of time and forward into eternity. Before we begin the descent and consider the practical implications, Romans 12:1 encourages us to take in the panorama one more time.

When we were condemned in *the valley of sin* and deserving of judgment, God stepped in. *The crux of salvation* is Jesus, crucified for our sins, so that we can be justified by faith. It's not through our good works but a gift of righteousness. The footsteps of Abraham then led us to *the place of peace*. We have free access to God and his love is poured into our hearts by the Spirit. We then followed *the ridge of freedom* that led up to *the summit of hope*. We are not condemned in sin. Having died with Christ, we are free to live a new life. The same Spirit who raised Jesus is alive in us. He adopts us into God's family and through him we cry, '*Abba*, Father!' We are co-heirs with Christ and a glorious inheritance awaits us – resurrection bodies in a perfectly restored creation. Now this gospel news is for all nations. As we saw in *the cloud of mystery*, it began with Israel, and one day they will return to their Messiah. In the meantime, we are heralds of hope. Nothing can separate us from the love of God!

After enjoying the view, it's time to begin our descent. On the way down, we will learn how to apply the gospel in practical ways throughout chapters 12—16. Remember, Romans is not just a letter to *look at* but a pair of spectacles to *look through* to make sense of life. With this in mind, please note that we are not going down the same way we came up. Instead, the goal is that we end up in a different place with a clearer perspective on life. A great adventure can do this for you as it alters your outlook. My prayer is that by the time we reach the other side of Romans, our confidence in the gospel will have increased, along with our ability to live it out in everyday life. So don't think of the descent as an anticlimax. After all, in the kingdom of God, the way down proves to be the way up. When we get on our knees and serve with humility, we discover true greatness. *The descent of devotion* will show us how this works in practice.

Part 1: Living sacrifices

In the opening verses (Rom. 12:1–2), Paul urges us not to conform to the values of the culture around us. Instead, we must offer our bodies in service to God.

Part 2: Loving servants

The rest of Romans 12 consists of short, staccato phrases that describe the Christian life. It's about loving God, serving others and overcoming evil with good.

> In view of God's mercy, offer your bodies as a living sacrifice, holy and pleasing to God.
>
> *Romans 12:1*

Part 1: Living sacrifices

READ: Romans 12:1–2

Imagine Phoebe reading the letter to the house churches in Rome. They've enjoyed the high-level vision of God's redemptive purpose. But now they want to know what it looks like down at street level, among the tenements, markets and forums of ancient Rome. So, after eleven chapters summarising what God has done, Paul now turns to what we do in response.

By the way, this is how the gospel works. In fact, this is how salvation works throughout the Bible. When Israel were enslaved in Egypt, God delivered them through the Exodus. Only then did he give them the Torah so they could live out their freedom. The gospel reflects this pattern. While we were still sinners, Christ died for us. He set us free from condemnation. Now in chapter 12, Paul shows us how to live out our freedom in practical ways:

In view of God's mercy [gospel]

    offer your bodies as a living sacrifice [response]

Therefore, I urge you, brothers and sisters, in view of God's mercy, to offer your bodies as a living sacrifice, holy and pleasing to God – this is your true and proper worship. Do not conform to the pattern of this world, but be transformed by the renewing of your mind. Then you will be able to test and approve what God's will is – his good, pleasing and perfect will.

Romans 12:1–2

The phrase 'offer your bodies as a living sacrifice' alludes to numerous pagan temples in ancient Rome, where people would bring animals and offerings to the gods. Meat from the sacrifices was then repurposed by butchers and enjoyed in homes and restaurants throughout the city. In Jerusalem, the Jewish temple was also a scene of sacrifice. Some animals were brought as sin or guilt offerings. However, other sacrifices were burnt offerings. They were not given to atone for sin but out of gratitude, as an act of worship to God. In this instance, no meat was kept back. The whole animal was devoted to the Lord as a costly sacrifice (see Leviticus 6). This may have been what Paul had in mind in Romans 12:1. Christ's sacrifice has fully atoned for our guilt and sin. However, in response, we are to devote the whole of our lives to God. Our worship is no longer *bringing* a sacrifice but *being* the sacrifice. We are 'living sacrifices', fully surrendered on the altar before God.

To hammer this home, Paul uses a word with shock value in his context: 'offer your *bodies* as a living sacrifice'. Greek philosophy, following Plato, considered the physical body to be a negative thing, a tomb or prison from which the soul needed to escape. According to this dualistic outlook, the gods were not interested in what you did with your body. Spirituality was a matter of the soul and the mind. Sadly, this view soon infiltrated Christian theology. Worship became focused on church 'services' and salvation was reduced to 'souls' escaping this physical world and going to heaven.

Many Christians today are still hampered by these ideas that have more to do with the philosopher Plato than the Apostle Paul. Instead, Romans 12 deliberately reframes our entire existence. Worship is not just a matter of songs and prayers. It's embodied, practical living that pleases God. Worship is about what I say with my tongue, what I watch with my eyes, what I think in my mind, where I go with my feet, how I conduct my sex life, how I steward my time and possessions. Eugene Peterson therefore paraphrases it, 'Take your every day, ordinary life – your sleeping, eating, going-to-work, and walking-around life – and place it before God as an offering' (v. 1, MSG). The fact that we are '*living* sacrifices' suggests this must be a continuous act of surrendering our whole selves to God. After all, the problem with living sacrifices is that they tend to wriggle off the altar!

Jesus himself taught and modelled practices of self-denial and self-discipline. Earlier in Romans, Paul urged us through the help of the Holy Spirit to 'put to death the misdeeds of the body' (8:13). For me, this means trying to resist the pressure to live as a consumer, refusing to indulge in forms of excess, whether food, drink or entertainment. Our bodies belong to God, not to Starbucks or Instagram. I find weekly disciplines like fasting from food, switching off social media for twenty-four hours, physically kneeling to pray, giving away a percentage of income, serving and volunteering . . . these practices remind me that I am not a free agent on a cultural binge to get happy. I am a servant of Jesus Christ, called to live for God's glory.

What would it mean to offer our whole beings to God?

WHAT I LISTEN TO ········

········ HOW I THINK

········ WHAT I SAY

£

WHAT I SPEND
MY MONEY ON

····· WHAT I WATCH

····· WHERE I GO

Verse 1 goes on to say that our goal is to be 'holy and pleasing to God'. *The descent of devotion* means consciously resisting the pressure to conform to *the way of the world*. Paul challenges us not to be governed by *nature* – the instincts, desires and passions within us – nor to surrender to *culture* – the narratives, values and pressures around us. Instead, we can reorder our lives to please God by living according to his purpose: 'Do not conform to the pattern of this world, but be transformed by the renewing of your mind' (12:2).

We are immersed in a predominantly post-Christian, secular culture, which exerts a strong influence on us. We are like the proverbial frog in the saucepan as it is slowly heated up. We are unaware of what's happening around us and the influence it exerts on the way we think. Immersed in a secular culture, we risk conforming and complying in subtle ways. Instead of discerning what's true according to Scripture, we all too easily take our lead from what everyone else is doing and adjust our opinions to whatever is deemed to be 'progressive'. A paraphrase of verse 2 highlights the risk: 'Don't let the world around you squeeze you into its own mould' (12:2, J. B. Phillips).

A former British Prime Minister, David Cameron, once

addressed the Houses of Parliament after a vote by the Church of England's Synod didn't go the way society expected. In response, Cameron asked, 'When is the church going to get with the programme?' Isn't that revealing? Culture has a programme of values and practices and the church is expected to get with it to avoid being 'old fashioned'.

However, society's programme keeps changing but God's word is constant and true. Former Bishop N. T. Wright responded brilliantly to David Cameron in an article that noted the irony. If the early Christians had simply 'got with the programme', values we now take for granted would never have shaped Western civilisation in the first place:

> The early Christians got a reputation for believing in all sorts of ridiculous things such as humility, chastity and resurrection, standing up for the poor and giving slaves equal status with the free. And for valuing women more highly than anyone else had ever done. People thought them crazy, but they stuck to their counter-cultural gospel. If the Church had allowed prime ministers to tell them what the 'programme' was, it would have sunk without trace in fifty years.[1]

The kindest thing Christians can do for society is not to conform to the pattern of this world. Instead, we are called to be agents of social and spiritual transformation by holding on to the radical truths of Scripture.

WE SHALL NOT ADJUST OUR BIBLE TO THE
AGE, BUT BEFORE WE HAVE DONE WITH
IT, BY GOD'S GRACE, WE SHALL HAVE
ADJUSTED THE AGE TO THE BIBLE.

C. H. Spurgeon[2]

Instead of being *conformed*, we are to be: '*transformed* by the renewing of your mind' (12:2, italics added). The Greek word for transformed (*metamorphoo*) gives our word 'metamorphosis'. Think of a caterpillar spinning the cocoon around itself and later emerging as a liberated butterfly. What a beautiful vision. God has high hopes for us caterpillars! So we must embrace the process of change, including putting an end to old patterns of behaviour.

Notice that this transformation all begins with the mind. The way we see ourselves and the world needs to change. As mentioned previously, humans consist of both hardware and software, bodies and minds. Real transformation begins when our software is reprogrammed according to God's truth. Then the hardware, our bodies, can please God as we practically express his values in the world. That's what this Romans adventure has been all about. As we get a clearer view of God's love and our new identity, we embrace a radically different lifestyle that reflects it.

SOW A THOUGHT, REAP AN ACTION;
SOW AN ACTION, REAP A HABIT;
SOW A HABIT, REAP A CHARACTER;
SOW A CHARACTER, REAP A DESTINY.[3]

Let's illustrate this by considering our bodies and in particular how we express our sexuality. Greco-Roman culture was highly sexualised, just like ours. They had their own forms of pornography and prostitution. In that context, Paul challenges the assumption that personal gratification is the goal of life. Instead, we are to control our bodies and offer them to God. That includes keeping sexual intimacy for marriage, avoiding pornography that fuels lust and seeking a partner who shares our faith so we can serve the Lord together.

As in the first century, the path of devotion is a radical route. Living sacrifices will need to make costly decisions, such as not acting on desires that might seem natural, losing popularity with others, ending a relationship that is wrong, or facing periods of unwanted singleness. This is where the rubber hits the road.

However, don't think Christianity is masochistic misery. The reason God's pattern safeguards sex for within the covenant of marriage is because this is still the best context in which loyal love is expressed and children are nurtured. Of course, in practice it's more complicated than this, and no family is perfect. But God loves us, despite all our mess, and he desires that we should flourish. Paul refers to God's 'good, pleasing and perfect will' for our lives (12:2). Notice the word 'pleasing'. God wants us to experience joy and fulfilment. After all, he invented romance and sex, family and friendship.

Since the dawn of time, humans have been deceived into thinking that God's way is restrictive. Perhaps you've experienced the painful fallout of going your own way? If so, don't lose heart. With Jesus, there's always a way back. Like a good satnav, he reroutes us when we get ourselves lost. God's grace starts where we're at, and gets us back on track.

Stepping back for a moment, I find it helpful to see how Paul's instruction in Romans 12:1–2 returns us to the start of the letter. Remember, in *the valley of sin*, Paul described the downward slope of sin when we misdirected our worship towards created things and end up with a distort (*adokimos*) mind (1:28). This is what happens when we conform to the pattern of the world rather than the pattern of God. However, Romans 12 is the antidote to Romans 1. In response to God's mercy, we can now direct our worship back to God. Then we will be transformed into his likeness as our renewed minds are able to understand and approve (*dokimazō*) God's perfect will. In Greek, the letter 'a' prefixed to a word reverses its meaning. So Paul's deliberate word play in 1:28 and 12:2 indicates that a renewed mind is the opposite of a distorted mind. Paul knows that when we worship and serve God with our whole beings, the dehumanising effects of idolatry are reversed and we are restored.

> IF THE FUNDAMENTAL PROBLEM OF THE HUMAN
> RACE WAS IDOLATRY AND CONSEQUENT WRONG
> BEHAVIOUR (1.18), PAUL WILL NOW SHOW THAT
> TRUE WORSHIP, OFFERING ONE'S WHOLE SELF TO
> GOD, LEADS TO GENUINELY HUMAN BEHAVIOUR.
> N. T. Wright and M. F. Bird[4]

Given all that is at stake, Paul therefore urges us in the strongest possible terms to follow God's pattern: 'I appeal to you' (ESV UK) or 'I plead with you' (NLT). It's an urgent matter of life and death. We must choose to be transformed by the renewing of our minds. In view of God's mercy, this is the most sensible thing to do. Paul refers to the decision as a 'reasonable' response to the gospel (12:1, KJV). The Greek word here is *logican* from which we get our word 'logic'. When we realise that Jesus gave up everything for us, it is a logical response to offer everything to him. Our small sacrifices are nothing compared to the ultimate price he paid for us.

C. T. Studd was an England cricket captain and member of a wealthy family. He was heir to a large inheritance worth approximately £29,000 back in the nineteenth century. But in 1855 he gave it all up to share the good news of Jesus in China. What was the reasoning behind such a costly decision? 'If Jesus

Christ be God, and he died for me, what sacrifice could be too great for me to make for him?"[5] That's the impeccable logic of Romans 12:1–2.

REFLECT: What would it mean for you to offer each aspect of your life more fully to God? What might be some of the costs and rewards?

◐◯ Part 2: Loving servants

READ: Romans 12:3–21

A few years ago, I took my son up a mountain in the Lake District. On the way back down, we stopped for a rest on the ridge high above the valley where our car was parked. From there, we could see other cars on the road below. They looked like toys, they were so small. As we watched, two cars approached each other from either side of a narrow bridge. They met in the middle, but neither was prepared to reverse. Soon we heard the distant sound of horns honking and doors slamming. As we watched this miniature stand-off unfold, we couldn't help but laugh. From our vantage point it seemed ridiculous to fall out over something so petty.

After urging us to become living sacrifices, the rest of Romans 12 calls us to be loving servants who put others first. 'In view of God's mercy', or, as J. B. Phillips puts it, 'with eyes wide open to the mercies of God', we are to avoid petty squabbles. Instead, we must 'live in harmony with one another' (12:16) – even if that means reversing, apologising and forgiving. In Romans 12, Paul applies these principles with two different sets of relationships in mind.

Loving servants in God's family: 12:3–13

The central idea of this section is captured in verse 10: 'Be devoted to one another in love [*philadelphia*].' This word literally means 'brotherly love'. It is a word that implies a family context. Through adoption by the Spirit, Christians are brothers and sisters in God's family. As siblings, we should therefore be devoted to one another. What does this look like in practice?

In verses 3–8 Paul urges the Christians in Rome to serve each other with the gifts God has given. He lists several examples of spiritual gifts. Some are more upfront, including prophecy, leadership and teaching. Others are practical gifts, such as giving, encouraging, serving. As loving servants, we are called to use whatever talents and abilities we have been given to serve God's people.

But how do we know what our primary gifts are? In my experience, it is a process of discovery that takes time. We must focus first on doing whatever is needed out of a simple desire to serve others. When I was a teenager, I was appointed to be a 'steward' in my local church, which basically meant putting the chairs out every Sunday. As it turned out, my team leader, Des, held a senior role within a prestigious investment bank. I didn't know what this meant at the time, but when a friend told me that he was a millionaire, I was shocked. The next time we were stacking chairs together, I asked, 'Why are *you* doing this?'

Des looked puzzled. He didn't even understand the question. 'Because they need putting out!' he replied.

Lesson learned. Regardless of our skill set or pay grade, we are called to be servants following the Master who washed his disciples' feet. The way up is the way down.

We begin to discover our gifts by serving in a more general way – multitasking. However, over time and through the feedback of others, our particular calling and gifts will reveal themselves. Then our contribution can be increasingly specialised as we receive training and grow in experience. So be patient. None of us is helicoptered to the top of the mountain. We work our way into our calling slowly but surely.

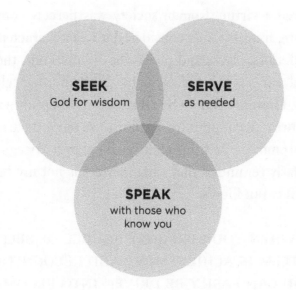

How to discover your God-given gifts

To reinforce the importance of using our gifts to serve, Paul draws on one of his favourite metaphors – the church is a collective *body* with many individual *parts*. This metaphor both encourages those who feel *inferior* – you have gifts and we need you to play your part – and it humbles those who feel *superior* – remember, you are only one part and need to honour others. In our modern culture of celebrities and pedestals, it's all too easy to become motivated by fame, wealth and accolades. TV programmes like *The X Factor* or *Britain's Got Talent* offer ordinary people the opportunity to become superstars through showcasing their talents on stage. This motivation can creep into the church. So in verse 3 Paul warns, 'Do not think of yourself more highly than you ought', and in verse 16, 'Do not be conceited.'

Instead, the New Testament is full of commands to use our gifts with humility. This may seem obvious to us – 'Of course it's good to be humble'. But in ancient Rome humility was not considered a virtue. Roman society was fiercely competitive. Therefore, humility was considered a weak character trait for social inferiors, slaves and plebs who should know their place. Yet Paul expects *all* believers to think of themselves with modesty. Humility should be a distinct, countercultural feature of the Christian community. We must use our gifts to serve, not to self-promote. I find this really challenging. My ego needs to be regularly reminded that what matters is not my reputation or notoriety but God's.

> WHEN YOUR PRIMARY SOURCE OF SELF-
> ESTEEM IS ACHIEVEMENT AND RECOGNITION,
> YOU CAN EASILY BE DRIVEN INTO BECOMING
> A WORKAHOLIC SHOW PONY, CONSTANTLY
> CRAVING ATTENTION AND ACCLAIM. SELF-
> CONGRATULATORY OVERACHIEVERS MAY
> EXUDE EXCESSIVE CONFIDENCE . . . BUT DEEP
> DOWN THEY ARE OFTEN INSECURE PEOPLE.
> Michael Bird[6]

In verses 9–13 Paul goes on to urge the Christians in Rome to develop healthy relationships marked by sincerity, generosity and hospitality. Sincerity is the opposite of hypocrisy. *Hypokrites* was a Greek word used for an actor who put on a show by hiding behind masks. Throughout the performance you never got to see the real person. So much human socialising is just two masks meeting. But the gospel says we are loved and accepted on the basis of who we really are, not who we pretend to be. So we can take off our masks and share our weakness and struggles. It's vulnerability that cultivates deep and meaningful relationships.

Paul also urges the practice of generosity and hospitality.

After all, when we were out in the cold, God paid the greatest price to bring us home. So, as Christians, we are to welcome strangers and meet the needs of others. When we invite someone into our home and share food together, we turn strangers into friends. In fact, the word 'companion' derives from the Latin *cum* (together) and *panis* (bread). We make companions as we eat together. When we show generosity and practise hospitality we put the gospel into practice. In a lonely world this can make a big difference. As the early Christians in Rome put Paul's teaching into practice, their kindness and generosity was soon noticed by the society around them. An early Christian leader in the second century described what non-Christians were saying about Christians in ancient Rome:

> See, they say, *how they love one another* (for they themselves are animated by mutual hatred); how they are ready even to die for one another (for they themselves will sooner put to death).
>
> *Tertullian*, c. AD *160*–c. AD *225*[7]

Loving servants of our enemies: 12:14–21

The final section of Romans 12 is the most radical. It's one thing to love and serve those who are on our side; it's another to extend this kindness to those who make life difficult for us – our enemies. Human instinct is to stand up for ourselves and to try to get our own back whenever possible. But the gospel calls us to live counter-intuitive lives. The final verse sums it up:

> Do not be overcome by evil but overcome evil with good.
>
> *Romans 12:21*

In order to get our heads round this radical teaching, we need to rewind to chapter 5 where Paul summed up how God has treated his enemies: 'while we were still sinners, Christ died for us' (5:8). When the human race turned its back on God, Jesus' back was lashed for us. When we took matters into our own hands, his hands were pierced for us. The crucifixion of Christ inaugurated a whole new paradigm, encapsulated in his prayer from the cross, 'Father, forgive them' (Luke 23:32). Romans 12 takes hold of the gospel that we have received and applies it to our treatment of others. If God loved us when we were his enemies, we ought to love our enemies and do good to those who hate us (Luke 6:27).

> BY SUFFERING VIOLENCE AS AN INNOCENT
> VICTIM, [JESUS] TOOK UPON HIMSELF THE
> AGGRESSION OF THE PERSECUTORS. HE
> BROKE THE VICIOUS CYCLE OF VIOLENCE BY
> ABSORBING IT, TAKING IT UPON HIMSELF.
> Miroslav Volf[8]

In Romans 12, Paul lets off a volley of phrases designed to reprogramme the way we respond to those who offend or harm us. As you read them, I wonder who comes to mind? Is there a colleague at work who deliberately undermines you, a church member who annoys you, a partner who deserted you, a parent who failed you? How do we respond to such experiences?

- Verse 14: 'Bless those who persecute you; bless and do not curse.'
- Verse 17: 'Do not repay anyone evil for evil.'

- Verse 20: 'If your enemy is hungry, feed him; if he is thirsty, give him something to drink.'
- Verse 21: 'Do not be overcome by evil, but overcome evil with good.'

The streets of ancient Rome were notoriously narrow and dangerous, with gangs roaming and thieves operating. Those to whom Phoebe was reading the letter would have been used to a dog-eat-dog world. In the absence of any police force, the only deterrent against assailants was to show strength and if necessary exact revenge. For a dramatised take on this revenge culture in ancient Rome, just watch the film *Gladiator*. But Paul calls the early Christians to be living sacrifices, to respond to hatred and violence in a countercultural manner. Revenge is simply not an option for those who have declared Jesus to be Lord. When hurt by someone, we must fight the temptation to act out revenge fantasies or escalate tensions. Instead, our calling is to overcome evil with good.

When you witness this countercultural forgiveness in real life, it stops you in your tracks. On 17 June 2015, a young white man called Dylann Roof entered a church in Charleston (USA) where some of the members had gathered for a Bible study. Though Dylann was a stranger, they greeted him warmly. However, he proceeded to take out a pistol and open fire. By the time he'd finished, nine Black parishioners were dead.

Less than forty-eight hours after the shooting, some of the victims' families spoke at Roof's first court appearance. Their words stunned the watching world: 'I forgive you,' said Nadine Collier, whose mother was killed. 'You took something very precious from me and I will never talk to her ever again . . . But

I forgive you. May God have mercy on your soul.' Another of the victims who survived the shooting said that Dylann would still be welcome at their Bible study so that he could discover God's love for himself.

Their response to such hatred had a profound impact on many. As one of the family members concluded, 'We have no room for hating . . . we have to forgive.'

Verse 20 of Romans 12 has left commentators debating what Paul meant ever since: 'If your enemy is hungry, feed him; if he is thirsty, give him something to drink. In doing this, you will heap burning coals on his head' (12:20). Some have interpreted this as exacting a form of revenge by taking the moral high ground and shaming your enemy. But the whole context suggests a more positive interpretation. Instead, it is more likely Paul is saying that, just as God's sacrificial love converted us from enemies to friends, so your counter-intuitive kindness has the power to do the same. In other words, the burning coals are a metaphor for purging, not destroying. This is not strictly a promise, but it is redemptive hope that should motivate us.

> A ROLE MODEL OF RECONCILIATION AND
> FORGIVENESS, [JESUS] STRETCHED OUT
> HIS HANDS IN LOVE, ACCEPTANCE AND
> HEALING. CHRIST'S EXAMPLE HAS TAUGHT
> ME TO SEEK TO RESPECT AND VALUE ALL
> PEOPLE OF WHATEVER FAITH OR NONE.
> Queen Elizabeth II[9]

The final verse of chapter 12 is a great note to end on: 'Do not be overcome by evil, but overcome evil with good' (12:21). We cannot defeat hatred with force. The Western world has recently been reminded that military aggression destroys lives and creates more enemies. Hate breeds hate. As Martin Luther King Jr famously said in a speech given during the civil rights campaign, 'Darkness cannot drive out darkness; only light can do that. Hate cannot drive out hate; only love can do that.'[10] Paul therefore urges us to leave retributive justice to God and the state.

On the final day of judgment, God will right all wrongs. In the meantime, he delegates his authority to human governments to administer justice on behalf of their citizens – more on that in Romans 13. But our focus should be on overcoming evil by repaying it with good. I love a mural by the mysterious graffiti artist Banksy, which he painted on a garage wall just outside Bethlehem in Israel. A masked man is about to hurl something at the enemy. But instead of a grenade, in his hand is a beautiful bunch of flowers. When we act in surprising ways and return kindness for hate, we follow the way of Christ and overcome evil with good.

'In view of God's mercy', Romans 12 urges us to become *living sacrifices* and *loving servants*. When I imagine what this looks like in practice, I think of my Aunty Edna who died a few years ago. She was truly a devoted follower of Jesus. During the week, she made clothes for emergency appeals, at her own expense. On Sundays, she walked many miles in order to lead groups for children in village churches nearby. One day when she was in her nineties, with eyesight failing, two thugs broke into her home at night and robbed her. After they had gone, she called my mother to explain what had happened. Her instinctive response? 'This is a real problem for me. I already had a long prayer list and now I have two more people to add to it!' From then on, Aunty Edna prayed for her enemies every day.

Years later, at her funeral, I got chatting to a man who turned out to be the chaplain at a nearby prison. The two thugs had both been caught and ended up under lock and key. But there in prison, one of them started attending chapel services where he heard the gospel. The grace of God worked through the prayers of Aunty Edna, and that young man became a devoted follower of Jesus! I think this is the sort of thing Paul had in mind when he wrote:

Do not be overcome by evil, but overcome evil with good.

REFLECT: What might it mean for you to 'overcome evil with good'? Is there someone you have been hurt by to whom you could show kindness?

Ask God for practical ways to respond to this teaching and the courage to act on it.

In view of God's mercy . . . offer your bodies as a living sacrifice, holy and pleasing to God.

Romans 12:1

9

The return to community

Romans 13:1—14:23

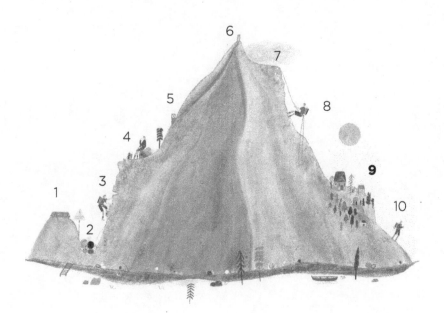

The return to community

Romans 13:1–14:23

My wife is the proud owner of two passports. She was born in the United Kingdom, but thanks to her American mother, Charlotte is also a citizen of the United States. Dual citizenship means she has rights and responsibilities in both realms. In Romans 13—14, Paul considers what it means for Christians to be dual citizens. After all, we were born in a physical country with a secular government, but we've also been born again into a spiritual realm where Christ is king. In my case, that makes me a citizen of the United Kingdom and of God's kingdom. How about you?

In Romans 13, Paul outlines our responsibilities as members of society. Then, in Romans 14, he considers our obligations to each other within the Christian community.

Before we dive in, it is important to understand how this notion of dual citizenship defied the status quo. In the ancient world, religion and government were completely intertwined. Part of being a good citizen involved worshipping the Roman gods. Political and religious allegiance went hand in hand. Even the emperor was worshipped. This was known as the imperial cult, with temples and sacrifices in his honour.[1]

In this context, Jesus introduced a radically different approach by carefully distinguishing God's kingdom from political rulers and nation states. Imagine him standing before Pontius Pilate, the Roman procurator, and declaring, 'My kingdom is not of this world' (John 18:36). According to the New Testament, God's kingdom and the Roman Empire may overlap for the time being, but they are two distinct realms. However, God is sovereign over both, and the book of Revelation envisages a day when, 'The kingdom of the world has become the kingdom of our Lord and of his Messiah, and he will reign for ever and ever' (Rev. 11:15). In the meantime, Christians are dual citizens with obligations to both society and church.

Getting the balance right between 'church' and 'state', between 'secular' and 'spiritual' authorities, is really important. Over the centuries, some have attempted to turn secular society into God's kingdom, with earthly rulers assuming spiritual authority over the church.[2] Others have gone to the opposite extreme, a form of separatism where Christians distance themselves from mainstream society as if the only kingdom they belong to is God's. This results in religious ghettos that fail to be salt and light in the world.

We can avoid both extremes, syncretism and separatism, when we appreciate what it means to be dual citizens. Romans 13—14 wrestle with the implications of this: *If our allegiance is to God, how do we relate to secular governments? What if they should forbid what God commands or command what God forbids? What if a politician sets rules and then breaks them? Are we still obliged to obey? Is civil disobedience an option for Christians?*

As we continue our descent from the summit, we must now prepare ourselves for community life. The final chapters of Romans give practical wisdom that applies the gospel to everyday life back home. *The return to community* will therefore equip us to play our part in secular society and in Christ's kingdom.

Part 1: How to be a godly citizen in a secular society

Romans 13 makes clear that we are obligated to the community and nation in which we live. So how can we obey secular authorities as well as live in a way that is countercultural?

Part 2: How to be a positive member of Christ's church

Romans 14 calls Christians to live in unity together even though we may disagree. What principles can help us work through our differences and show the world that we are one?

> The kingdom of God is not a matter of eating and drinking, but of righteousness, peace and joy in the Holy Spirit.
>
> *Romans 14:17*

Part 1: How to be a godly citizen in a secular society

READ: Romans 13:1–14

Last Christmas I received an unusual present – a first-century Roman coin, called a denarius. My children have already called me a 'geek', so you can keep that thought to yourself! The coin is particularly interesting because it bears the image of Emperor Tiberius, who reigned AD 14–37. The coin would therefore have been in circulation when Jesus lived in Roman-occupied Palestine.

On one occasion, the Pharisees asked Jesus whether as God's people it was still necessary to pay taxes to Rome. Faced with this dilemma, Jesus said, 'Bring me a *denarius* and let me look at it' (Mark 12:15, italics added). Now do you appreciate the significance of my coin? It's the same one Jesus held. Well, the same edition at least – a silver denarius, also known as a 'tribute penny',[3] equivalent to one day's wage for a skilled worker – about £150 today.

Image of my Denarius coin

Holding the coin before the crowd, Jesus famously asked, "'Whose image is this?' ... "Caesar's," they replied. Then Jesus said to them, "Give back to Caesar what is Caesar's and to God what is God's'" (Mark 12:16–17).

There you have it, dual citizenship. Caesar's image is on the coin, so pay taxes to him. But if the image of God is stamped all over you, devote yourself to God. Brilliant!

But what does this mean in practice? What do Christian citizens owe to earthly authorities? Romans 13 gives the most sustained answer in the Bible. Paul echoes Jesus' teaching and fills in some extra detail:

> Let everyone be subject to the governing authorities, for there is no authority except that which God has established. The authorities that exist have been established by God ... For the one in authority is God's servant for your good.
>
> *Romans 13:1, 4*

Paul affirms two fundamental truths that have radical implications. First, rulers on earth are ultimately ordained by God in heaven. Regardless of whether they gain office by democratic vote or through hereditary rights, 'there is no authority except that which God has established'. In a certain sense, God delegates his own authority to secular rulers. However, notice Paul does not mention any rulers by name. He is not endorsing particular individuals, but rather he considers civil authority to be an expression of God's grace and a means of securing the common good. So, regardless of what we made of Angela Merkel, Barack Obama or Tony Blair, we should respect the position they held.

> GOVERNMENT IS MORE THAN A NUISANCE
> TO BE PUT UP WITH; IT IS AN INSTITUTION
> ESTABLISHED BY GOD TO ACCOMPLISH
> SOME OF HIS PURPOSES ON EARTH.
> Douglas Moo[4]

Second, an earthly ruler is 'God's servant' (13:4), whether they realise it or not. In the Old Testament, pagan authorities like Nebuchadnezzar (Daniel 3:28) and Cyrus (Isaiah 45:1) were referred to as instruments in God's hands. Paul builds on this tradition but takes it a step further. In referring to secular rulers as 'servants' (*diakonoi*), Paul uses a word that elsewhere describes 'deacons' or 'ministers' in the church. The implication is that political leaders are God's servants in a similar way to church leaders. As with the example of Judas mentioned earlier, being *chosen to serve* is not the same thing as being *chosen for salvation*. Nevertheless, civil leaders are 'servants of God' in this life, whether or not Winston Churchill, Margaret Thatcher or Nelson Mandela realised it.

It should be no surprise, therefore, that Paul calls Christians to submit themselves to secular authorities – even bad ones. After all, as we have learned from recent conflicts, including in Iraq and Syria, removing a dictator can result in brutal sectarian violence. This is why the New Testament generally favours the idea of government (Titus 3:1; 1 Pet. 2:13–14). As Christians, our obedience to 'Caesar' is considered to be an extension of our obedience to God.

> I AM DISTURBED BY PAUL'S TEACHING THAT THE
> AUTHORITY OF THIS AGE AND THE JUDGMENT
> OF THE WORLD ARE MINISTERS OF GOD.
> Origen (c.184–253)[5]

This teaching must have sounded challenging to those Phoebe originally met with in Rome. Around the time Paul wrote Romans, Nero became emperor. His psychotic tendencies were notorious. Allegedly, he kicked his own wife to death. Soon the early Christians became a target as he blamed them for starting the Great Fire of Rome (AD 64). Many were slaughtered as scapegoats. In that political context, should Christians really 'be subject to the governing authorities'? Is even Nero 'God's servant'? It's easier to accept Paul's teaching while living in a relatively stable democratic society, but for Christians who live under corrupt regimes today, Romans 13 raises some knotty questions.

In his book, *Reading While Black*, Esau McCaulley reflects on Romans 13 from the perspective of a person of colour and in the light of recent instances of police brutality.[6] How do we hold to Paul's teaching in a world marred by injustice, racism and oppression? While the challenge of Romans 13 must not be avoided, some qualifying points seem necessary in the light of the wider teaching of Scripture.

First, as dual citizens, we may have two passports, but our allegiance to God always takes priority. Therefore, if an earthly ruler uses their position to command something God forbids, or to forbid something God commands, we must obey God. Now, I am not referring to relatively trivial matters that we can accommodate. During the coronavirus lockdowns, when the UK government forbade church congregations from singing to help prevent the spread of the virus, I heard of a few churches who defied the rule on the basis that the Bible commands Christians to sing. I'm not convinced this was necessary, especially during a public health crisis. However, where governments more directly forbid the communication of the gospel, Christian obedience may necessitate civil disobedience. After all, in Romans 9, Paul recalled the moment when Moses stood toe to toe with Pharaoh and demanded that he release the Hebrew slaves and end their oppression. In the New Testament, the apostles boldly declared to Jewish authorities, 'We must obey God rather than human beings!' (Acts 5:29).

> PROTEST IS NOT UNBIBLICAL; IT IS A
> MANIFESTATION OF OUR ANALYSIS OF THE
> HUMAN CONDITION IN LIGHT OF GOD'S OWN
> WORD AND VISION FOR THE FUTURE.
> Esau McCaulley[7]

Second, being a good citizen means not allowing powerful rulers to exploit the weak and vulnerable. While respecting those in authority, we should campaign for values like equality and human rights and we should protest against injustice and oppression. Christians have often been at the forefront of resistance movements – think of William Wilberforce, Harriet Tubman or Martin Luther King.

By the way, if you don't know who Harriet Tubman is, why not watch the film *Harriet* (2019) or read her biography by Catherine Clinton.[8] As a Black slave in nineteenth-century Southern America, Harriet was beaten so badly by her masters that she sustained severe head injuries. However, some friends helped her to escape north through the 'underground railroad'. When she reached Pennsylvania, she was so grateful to be free that she went back to rescue her family. At great risk, she kept going back to liberate more and more people. Harriet successfully completed thirteen undercover raids, rescuing more than seventy slaves.

As a Christian, Harriet used her freedom to save many others. Her conviction was so compelling, even one of the guards sent to capture her joined the mission! As Harriet herself said, 'I have heard their groans and sighs, and seen their tears, and I would give every drop of blood in my veins to free them . . . I said to the Lord, I'm going to hold steady on to you, and I know you will see me through'.[9]

Photograph of Harriet Tubman (1822–1913)

In some contexts today it is necessary for Christians to break the law in order to share the gospel or distribute Bibles. On very rare occasions, use of force may even be justified in order to end an evil regime. For example, Dietrich Bonhoeffer was a Christian leader in Germany during the Second World War. He publicly opposed the Nazis and contributed to a failed attempt to assassinate Hitler. Did that contradict Romans 13, or might extreme circumstances warrant such action? A Scottish theologian called Samuel Rutherford (1600–61) published a political tract called *Lex Rex* ('Law is King') in which he argued that, on rare occasions, resistance to tyrannical rulers is justified. If, like me, you are undecided, try a thought experiment: imagine you found yourself in Nazi Germany in 1939 and someone offered you a sniper's rifle with Adolf Hitler in the sights. Could you pull the trigger in good conscience? Tricky.

IF YOU ARE NEUTRAL IN SITUATIONS
OF INJUSTICE, YOU HAVE CHOSEN
THE SIDE OF THE OPPRESSOR.
Archbishop Desmond Tutu[10]

Finally, it is worth noting that some Christians may find themselves in the difficult predicament of working for corrupt governments or institutions. It's easy to judge from a distance and assume that they are complicit with the evil. But things are not always as they seem. During the Second World War, Colonel Alexis Baron Von Roenne was a senior intelligence officer who reported directly to Hitler. However, unbeknown to both the Nazis and the Allies, Von Roenne was a Christian who had decided to undermine the evil regime from within. When the Allied forces devised a deception plan to convince Hitler that their invasion would happen further south, German officers suspected it to be bogus. However, Von Roenne presented the intelligence to Hitler as credible and managed to convince him to move troops away from Normandy.

When Hitler realised he had been deceived, he ordered Von Roenne's execution. On 11 October 1944 he was bound hand and foot and hung by the neck from a meat hook until he died. On the eve of his death, Von Roenne wrote a moving note to his wife: 'In a moment now I shall be going home to our Lord in complete calm and in the certainty of salvation.'[11] Who would have thought that a senior Nazi intelligence officer was serving Christ in such a brave manner? Note to self: do not judge. You rarely know the full story.

In the light of these qualifiers, let's return to the question at hand: *What does it mean to be a good citizen in a secular society?*

Romans 13 gives three simple instructions:

1. Respect authorities: verses 1–5

As we've seen, the basic disposition of a Christian towards those in authority, whether politicians, civil servants or law-enforcement officers, is to be one of honour and respect. Today, this could include driving within the speed limit, adhering to health and safety legislation, and obeying rules and restrictions even if we disagree with them. Elsewhere, Paul urges Christians to regularly pray for 'kings and all those in authority' (1 Tim. 2:1–2). We must also be careful to avoid criticising or slandering those in leadership. Today, many conspiracy theories and rumours circulate on social media. However, as good citizens, we should give our leaders the benefit of the doubt until or unless it becomes clear that trust has been broken.

Paul also notes that secular authorities 'bear the sword' and 'bring punishment on the wrongdoer' (13:4). This was not so much an endorsement of capital punishment but a reference to those charged with law enforcement in ancient Rome. This sprawling, chaotic city was 'policed' by vigilante groups who often took matters into their own hands. But Paul urges Christians to trust the authorities to administer justice.

We also have a duty to report potential crimes and not to shield those being investigated. Recent revelations of Christians failing to report possible child abuse or safeguarding issues reinforces the need to understand our responsibilities as dual citizens. Criminal cases are not to be handled by the church since God has entrusted authority to the state for such matters.

2. Contribute to the good of society: verses 6–10

In verse 7, Paul specifically calls on Christians to provide 'revenue' for the state and to fully participate in public life. This echoes the Old Testament prophet Jeremiah who, when Israel were exiled in pagan Babylon, urged them to 'seek the peace and prosperity of the city' (Jer. 29:7). Regardless of how pagan or secular society becomes, Christians are called to contribute to the common good. The most obvious way to do this is to pay taxes as required by the government (13:6). This is every bit as spiritual as giving to the church or to charity.

Paul also instructs Christians to avoid financial debt and to live within their means so they can contribute to the needs of others and not become a burden. This includes promptly paying bills and invoices and not allowing consumer debt to build up. After all, as good citizens, we want to be in a position to support those who are struggling. Paul therefore goes on to say, 'Let no debt remain outstanding, except the continuing debt to love one another' (13:8). The fulfilment of God's law is not just about staying out of trouble ('adultery', 'murder', 'stealing': 13:9). It's also about radical generosity that cares for the needs of others.

The kind of debt Paul has in mind in verse 8 is inspiring, not crippling. It sends us out every day with a mandate to show kindness to everyone in Jesus' name. I recently met a young doctor called Ed who works two days a week in a London hospital. The rest of his time and money he uses to lead an organisation that is sharing God's love in practical ways all across India. In particular, the organisation feels a special debt of love for those at the bottom of the caste system. As a result of his radical devotion to the poor, Ed may not own a house or wear expensive clothes, but he radiates a deep joy. He feels a debt of love to the last, the least and the lost, which is utterly compelling.

> THE DEBT OF CHARITY SHOULD BE WITH
> US ALWAYS AND NEVER CEASE. WE MUST
> PAY THIS DAILY AND ALWAYS OWE IT.
> Origen (c.184–253)[12]

3. Live in the light of Christ: verses 11–14

This morning I got up early and climbed to the top of a hill to watch the sunrise. Initially, the sky was pitch black, but slowly things began to change. With every passing minute, the horizon was filled with more light as the new day dawned. At the end of Romans 13, Paul uses the metaphor of sunrise to capture the situation we find ourselves in as Christian citizens: 'The night is nearly over; the day is almost here. So let us put aside the deeds of darkness and put on the armour of light' (13:12). Society around us may be lost in darkness but, as Christians, we know that a new day is about to dawn. As followers of Jesus, we therefore experience spiritual jet lag. The world around us lies in darkness, but we are in a different time zone where dawn is already breaking. God's purpose of salvation includes the promise of a fully restored creation in which resurrected humans will flourish in God's glory. One day, there will be no more taxes or speed limits, no more suffering or pain, no more poverty or death. In the meantime, we are living in the dark interval just before sunrise. Here we are called to herald the dawn by shining as brightly as possible.

WE ARE TO BUILD OUR LIVES ON ETERNAL
THINGS, THE THINGS THAT LAST — TRUTH,
GOD, LOVE, RIGHTEOUSNESS. WE ARE TO
IMAGINE THAT THE DAY HAS DAWNED AND
THAT JESUS IS RIGHT BEFORE US, AND THEN
ASK: NOW, HOW WOULD I BEHAVE?
Tim Keller[13]

Paul goes on to explain what this means in practice:

> Let us behave decently, as in the daytime, not in carousing and
> drunkenness, not in sexual immorality and debauchery, not in
> dissension and jealousy. Rather, clothe yourselves with the
> Lord Jesus Christ, and do not think about how to gratify the
> desires of the flesh.
>
> *Romans* 13:13–14

The Romans were famous for hosting *symposia* or drinking
parties that quickly became drunken orgies. Paul urges
Christians instead to live in the light. Today, it's easy to succumb
to the culture around us until we eat, spend, drink, watch, flirt,
consume and indulge like everyone else. To be good citizens in
a secular society, we must refuse to compromise with the darkness and instead shine the light of Christ.

On my eighteenth birthday, my youth leader gave me a card
in which he had written out Romans 13:14: 'Clothe yourselves
with the Lord Jesus Christ, and do not think about how to gratify the desires of the flesh.' Later that day, friends came round
to celebrate and we started watching a film. After a few minutes
there was a scene with some nudity that made me feel uncomfortable. But what could I do? After a few more minutes it
happened again, only this time more explicitly. As I squirmed

in silence, Romans 13 came strongly to mind: 'Clothe your-selves with the Lord Jesus Christ, and do not think about how to gratify the desires of the flesh.' With a jolt I came to my senses. I walked over to the TV, switched it off and said, 'I don't want to watch this on my birthday.' After an awkward silence, we found something more positive to do. Stepping out of the shadows into the light can be a hard thing to do. But that day I drew a line in the sand and set the course for my adult life.

Are you hiding in darkness or living for the new day? Why not begin each morning on your knees as the sun rises and make a conscious decision to 'clothe yoursel[f] with the Lord Jesus Christ' (13:14). Then we will fulfil our responsibilities as Christian citizens – respecting those in authority, contributing to the good of society and shining the light of Christ.

REFLECT: In which of the following ways could you contribute more to your community?

- Volunteer for a local charity
- Pick up litter in a community space
- Check on a lonely neighbour
- Pay taxes and invoices promptly
- Follow health and safety guidelines (including the speed limit!)
- Donate to a food bank or charity
- Offer hospitality to neighbours and those in need
- Other: _____

○○ Part 2: How to be a positive member in Christ's church

READ: Romans 14:1–23

As dual citizens, it's time to pick up our other passport and consider what it means to participate fully in God's kingdom. In particular, Romans 14 outlines instructions to safeguard unity among the Roman house churches. Remember, Phoebe would have read the letter to several gatherings across the city of Rome, in both wealthy villas and rough workshops. Either way, New Testament letters like Romans were written to Christians who met together regularly. This reminds us that to be a Christian means being part of the church. I'm not talking about attending religious services but belonging to a community of God's people. After all, God is our Father and we are adopted brothers and sisters. Like any family, it can be complicated and at times frustrating. Nevertheless, we are called to play an active part as members of Christ's church.

In Romans 14, Paul's primary concern is that the house churches don't fragment into ghettos of Jewish and Roman Christians who mistrust one another. In particular, cultural issues such as meat eating vs. vegetarianism, drinking alcohol vs. teetotalism were becoming points of division. Listen to the opening verses of the chapter to get a feel for what was at stake:

Accept the one whose faith is weak, without quarrelling over disputable matters. One person's faith allows them to eat anything, but another, whose faith is weak, eats only vegetables. The one who eats everything must not treat with contempt the

one who does not, and the one who does not eat everything
must not judge the one who does, for God has accepted them.

Romans 14:1–3

The specific issues may seem less relevant now. However, the
general principles that Paul outlines here remain vital. When
Paul mentions 'strong' and 'weak' Christians, he does not mean
the strength of their faith or spiritual courage. Rather, he is referring to the fact that some people have more sensitive consciences
than others. This may be a result of personal temperament,
parental upbringing, theological convictions or cultural condi-
tioning. Either way, these basic differences surface regularly.

During the Covid-19 pandemic, I wonder if your friends or
colleagues were divided on how to interpret government guidelines. In my wider family, there were certainly some differences
regarding how cautious we should be. It led to moments of
tension as we interpreted the same events differently. Perhaps
you've witnessed similar disagreements between those who are
more socially conservative and others who are more liberally
minded? Differences regarding the sorts of music, books and
films we feel able to enjoy, how much alcohol we drink or what
clothes or make-up we wear. Christian relationships can also be
strained by theological differences on a whole range of issues,
from the age of the earth to the return of Christ.

Romans 14 reminds us that these sorts of tensions have been
around for millennia and are not going away. So we must learn
to handle them in a mature way so that our differences do not
undermine our unity. How can we achieve this?

First, it is important to note that *God's goal for the church is
unity, not uniformity*. Christianity was and is incredibly diverse
precisely because the gospel is so inclusive. Remember the list
of people Paul greeted at the conclusion of the letter (Romans

16)? It includes wealthy masters and uneducated slaves, Messianic Jews and ex-pagans, women and men, Europeans and Africans. So our aim is to build a *culture of acceptance within communities marked by difference*. This means getting comfortable with the fact that we won't all dress the same or see eye-to-eye . . . and that's OK!

Paul does not try to change anyone's mind in this section of the letter. He doesn't care who eats meat or who's vegetarian. That's not the point. Rather, it's about nurturing relationships of trust, love and acceptance. This is expressed most clearly in Romans 15:7: 'Welcome one another as Christ has welcomed you' (ESV UK).

I find this approach really liberating. The fact that I don't need to persuade you towards my opinion takes the pressure off both of us. It allows me to listen more openly and you to speak more honestly without feeling threatened by our differences. Remember, the goal is unity, not uniformity.

> GOD'S VISION FOR HIS PEOPLE IS NOT
> FOR THE ELIMINATION OF ETHNICITY
> TO FORM A COLORBLIND UNIFORMITY
> OF SANCTIFIED BLANDNESS.
> Esau McCaulley[14]

Second, *we need to distinguish between primary and secondary matters*. Without this distinction, an emphasis on acceptance could collapse into spiritual relativism – *it doesn't matter what we believe so long as we love each other*. Clearly, this is not the whole truth. In one of his other letters, Galatians, Paul vehemently opposed the idea that circumcision was essential to justification. He even dared the 'circumcision party' to go all the way and castrate themselves. Now that's a party you don't want to join!

Why did this issue invoke such a hostile reaction compared to other matters like food and drink in Romans 14? The clue is in the opening verse where Paul refers to 'disputable matters' or matters of conscience (Rom. 14:1). Whereas in Galatians gospel issues were at stake regarding who was 'in' and 'out' and on what basis, in Romans 14 the issues were not core to the gospel but matters of conscience. Paul therefore adopts a more gentle and open approach.

This reminds us that some truths are so clearly revealed in Scripture that they form a basis of unity for all Christians. In the context of Romans, this might include Paul's teaching on sin (chapters 1—2), atonement (chapter 3), justification by faith (chapter 4), freedom in Christ (chapters 5—7), eternal hope (chapter 8). But Romans 14 reminds us that other issues are matters of conscience. In Romans, this might include the future of Israel (Romans 9—11), use of spiritual gifts (Romans 12) or debates regarding pacifism and just war theory (Romans 13).

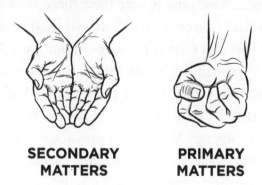

SECONDARY MATTERS   **PRIMARY MATTERS**

Following Paul's example, I find it helpful to organise theological differences into two main categories. Think of them as an open hand and a closed hand. Issues of secondary importance or 'disputable matters' (14:1) should be placed in the open hand. We can agree to disagree on these since they are not core to the gospel and different interpretations arise from Scripture. Personally, I would include among these: *the age of the earth, the nature of the sacraments (baptism and the Lord's Supper), the role of men and women, the sequence of events before the return of Christ, different worship styles.* I put these in the open hand, not because they are unimportant but because Bible-believing, Spirit-filled Christians think differently about them. On such 'disputable matters' (14:1) we must be careful not to allow our personal convictions to become divisive.

However, other issues are of primary importance and belong in the closed hand. In 1 Corinthians 15:3, Paul refers to the things of 'first importance' and goes on to mention the death, burial and resurrection of Jesus. We could add to this other core Christian doctrines, which are summarised in the Nicene Creed and the Apostles' Creed. They have been a source of unity across all major Christian traditions (Orthodox, Catholic, Protestant) for centuries.

Of course, the real skill is to place the correct issues in the open and closed hands and to keep them there. If we allow open-handed issues into the closed hand, we may become intolerant of alternative views and restrict the scope of our unity. However, if we move closed-handed issues into the open hand, we risk undermining our confidence in the gospel, which is equally dangerous. After all, some issues are not about 'weak' vs. 'strong' but 'right' vs. 'wrong'. We need to pray for the wisdom of the Holy Spirit and follow the guidance of the historic church, which has been negotiating these tensions for centuries.

It is also good to reflect on the influences that have shaped our attitude toward other Christians. For example, if you experienced a strict upbringing where every theological issue was black and white, it's easy to inherit a mistrust of others. This only reinforces itself if we congregate in echo chambers where everyone reads the same books and listens to the same podcasts. In my experience, having been raised in a Protestant context, it was incredibly humbling to realise that so many great theologians and godly people were Catholic! These experiences have helped me to adopt a more accommodating attitude to those who think differently on some matters.

> ## ON THE ESSENTIALS, UNITY; ON
> ## THE NON-ESSENTIALS, FREEDOM;
> ## IN EVERYTHING, LOVE.
> Rupertus Meldenius[15]

With these principles established, Paul gives specific instructions to 'strong' and 'weak' believers in order to safeguard a culture of acceptance. First, Paul urges the strong not to allow their exercise of freedom to become a 'stumbling-block' to the weak (14:13). Many of the 'strong' would have been Roman Christians, without any Jewish cultural background. Now notice that in calling them 'strong', Paul is affirming their convictions that no meat or drink is 'unclean' since God made all things good. To the Romans, this affirmation would have been good news! However, Paul then challenges the assumption that just because in principle we *could* do something means that in practice we *should* do it:

> All food is clean, but it is wrong for a person to eat anything that causes someone else to stumble. It is better not to eat meat or drink wine or to do anything else that will cause your brother or sister to fall.
>
> *Romans 14:20–1*

In our individualistic culture, Paul's teaching is challenging.

There are times when *I* must go without what *I* want in order to protect *our* unity. Instead of exercising personal freedom in a selfish way, my first priority is to safeguard those with a weaker conscience. For example, if I am with someone who does not drink alcohol for personal reasons, then perhaps I should choose a soft drink? If I am spending time with friends and we decide to watch a film, we should choose one that doesn't disturb anyone's conscience rather than my preferred choice. Or if a friend takes cannabis for medical purposes, I may need to get over that and not judge them as if it's a gospel issue.

> ## LOVE LIMITS ITS OWN LIBERTY OUT
> ## OF RESPECT FOR OTHERS.
> John Stott[16]

Paul also addresses those with a 'weak' conscience. In their case, he wants them to resist the pressure to conform out of fear of others because this will only lead them to feel guilty. As Paul concludes, 'whoever has doubts is condemned if they eat, because their eating is not from faith; and everything that does not come from faith is sin' (14:23). Have you ever done something that you weren't comfortable with because others wanted you to? This is such a weak way to live. It fails to glorify God and erodes self-respect. Instead, Paul urges everyone to act out of faith and conviction, not doubt or fear. This means only doing or saying things that would be appropriate if Jesus were standing next to us. Everything must be done to the glory of God.

If one danger for the weak is to conform out of fear, the other is to become critical of others. The 'weak' believers in Rome would have been mostly Jewish Christians who grew up with many customs and laws that were part of the Hebrew Scriptures.

No doubt they struggled with the idea that Roman believers were fully accepted apart from these laws, simply through faith in the Messiah. They were therefore in danger of becoming judgmental and critical of others. Paul confronts this attitude as he knows it erodes trust and unity: 'why do you judge your brother or sister? Or why do you treat them with contempt?' (14:10). It's one thing for us to decide that we cannot in good conscience drink whisky, wear make-up or watch certain films, but it's another to put that on everyone else. If I feel the need to abstain, I should do so to the glory of God. However, I must avoid making others feel guilty in the process. God will judge his servants; that's not my job. So, Paul says, 'stop passing judgment on one another' (14:13).

> THE MOST IMPORTANT THING IS TO
> MAKE SURE THE MOST IMPORTANT THING
> REMAINS THE MOST IMPORTANT THING.
> Old German Proverb

According to Romans 14, when it comes to secondary matters, it is far more important to be united than to be right. You may win an argument, but what if in the process you lose a brother or sister for whom Christ died? When we elevate matters of conscience to tests of orthodoxy, we undermine the gospel and sow seeds of division. This results in a cancel-culture where those who don't tick our boxes are viewed with suspicion and ostracised. Instead of being a place of radical acceptance, we form ghettos and cliques that are defensive and critical.

This is the opposite of God's vision for the church. Christ died in order to welcome the stranger home and to reconcile enemies as friends. Paul therefore implores the Roman Christians, 'Let us . . . make every effort to do what leads to peace and to mutual edification' (14:19). When we focus on the core truths of the gospel, we realise that so much more unites us than should ever divide us. We are forgiven by the blood of Christ, adopted through the Holy Spirit and loved by our heavenly Father. So what does it matter if we hold different convictions on secondary issues or prefer alternative styles of music?

As we head down the mountain and *return to community*, let's not lose sight of the bigger picture. 'In view of God's mercy' we are one in Christ, even though we're not the same. What matters is that we avoid unnecessary divisions and protect our God-given unity at all costs. Then we will enjoy life in community together. Romans 14:17 sums it up beautifully:

For the kingdom of God is not a matter of eating and drinking, but of righteousness, peace and joy in the Holy Spirit.

REFLECT:

- Which do you most identify with: a 'strong' conscience that is less sensitive, or a 'weak' conscience that is easily troubled?
- If 'strong', ask God to show you how you need to accommodate your freedoms to support others.
- If 'weak', ask God to help you follow your convictions and not to judge others who see things differently.

> The kingdom of God is not a matter of eating and drinking, but of righteousness, peace and joy in the Holy Spirit.
>
> *Romans 14:17*

10

The onward mission

Romans 15—16

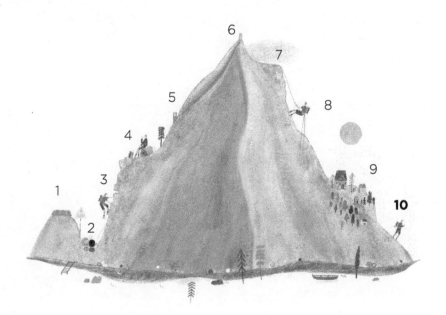

It is a well-known fact that most accidents occur on the way down a mountain. This is partly owing to physical exhaustion. However, the sheer elation of reaching the summit can also cause climbers to lose concentration just when they need it most. One false step on steep ground can be fatal. Edward Whymper learned this the hard way. In 1865, he led a team that achieved the first ever ascent of the Matterhorn in Switzerland. Imagine how they must have felt, standing on the summit of this awesome peak. However, within an hour, their joy had turned to tragedy. While crossing steep, icy slopes, a careless slip by an inexperienced climber sent four men hurtling to their death, still roped together.

> CLIMB IF YOU WILL, BUT REMEMBER THAT
> COURAGE AND STRENGTH ARE NOUGHT
> WITHOUT PRUDENCE . . . DO NOTHING IN HASTE;
> LOOK WELL TO EACH STEP; AND FROM THE
> BEGINNING THINK WHAT MAY BE THE END.
> Edward Whymper[1]

Our adventure through the letter to the Romans is almost over. We have climbed one of the highest peaks in the Bible and enjoyed spectacular views. However, I urge you to concentrate for this final section. It is vital that we complete the last stage of the route. Not only our spiritual lives but also the success of our mission depends on our arriving home, ready to apply all that we have learned.

Remember how this adventure started? We set off with a desire to grow in spiritual confidence so we could say with Paul, in the face of rival empires and philosophies, 'I am not ashamed of the gospel, because it is the power of God that brings salvation' (1:16). The goal was never simply to read Romans but to make sense of life through it. With this in mind, Paul concludes the letter by revealing ambitious plans to take the good news of Jesus further into Western Europe. Romans 15—16 have therefore posed a question to readers ever since: *What might it mean for you to make ambitious plans to share the gospel?* This final section of the descent is no time to relax or ease off. If Romans has done for you what it did for Saint Augustine, Martin Luther, John Wesley, Harriet Tubman, Hien Pham or David Suchet, then the real adventure is only just beginning!

 ## Part 1: The adventure continues . . .

Through Romans 15 we consider Paul's motivation and method for sharing the gospel, even when it got him into trouble. What can we do practically to share the good news of Jesus today?

○─○ Part 2: The ground we've covered

In this section we will step back and reflect on our adventure as a whole. How can we live 'in view of God's mercy, (12:1) as we return to everyday life?

Now to him who is able to establish you in accordance with my gospel . . . to the only wise God be glory for ever through Jesus Christ! Amen.

Romans 16:25, 27

Part 1: The adventure continues . . .

READ: Romans 15:1–33

Paul's passion for mission was unrelenting. By the time he dictated his letter to the Romans, he had already clocked up some impressive stats, and this before Google maps and budget flights.

- Travelled approximately 10,000 miles
- Preached the gospel from Jerusalem, through modern-day Turkey and round to Greece
- Planted more than ten churches
- Written more than ten foundational letters
- Spent years in prison
- Built a network of loyal friends across the Empire

Now, as Paul scoped his next missional move while resting in Corinth, his plans were even more ambitious. In Romans 15, Paul makes clear that he intends to travel to Jerusalem to deliver a gift he has collected for Jewish believers who are in a state of severe poverty. For Paul, this fundraising project was a symbolic gesture of something deeper: 'if the Gentiles have shared in the Jews' spiritual blessings, they owe it to the Jews to share with them their material blessings' (15:27). After visiting Jerusalem, Paul intended to sail to Rome, where he would finally meet the recipients of his great letter for the first time. He was clearly excited by the prospect and asked them to pray for safety, 'so that I may come to you with joy, by God's will, and in your company be refreshed' (15:32). Then Paul would head to southern Spain to open up a new frontier of mission. (I rather fancy that gig myself!)

I find Paul's plans in Romans 15 rather haunting because, from other sources, we know what actually happened. Paul made it to Jerusalem and delivered the financial gift. But then he was falsely accused of sacrilege in the temple and arrested by the Jewish authorities. After an attempt to assassinate him, he was moved up the coast to Caesarea Maritima, where he was kept behind bars for two years (see Acts 23—24). As a last roll of the dice, Paul claimed his right as a Roman citizen to be tried by Caesar. So, finally, he set sail for Rome as planned . . . Only, it didn't go to plan. His vessel was shipwrecked in a storm off the island of Malta. Paul and the other passengers made it to land, only for a poisonous viper to latch on to his arm! Needless to say, he miraculously survived. Finally, after months of further delay, around AD 58 Paul entered Rome as a political prisoner under house arrest (see Acts 27—28). Not quite what he had in mind when he shared his plans in Romans 15.

Have you noticed that life doesn't always go to plan? Even when we are serving Christ and on mission for God, unexpected things happen. Instead of arriving in Rome a free man, ready to launch the Western front into Spain, Paul arrived in chains. He must have felt confused – *why did God allow this to happen?* He must have felt a sense of despair – *how can anything good come from this?* These are the dark moments we all face from time to time. And this is where reality hits. Now the recipients of Paul's letter, the early Christians in Rome, would discover first-hand whether Paul really practised what he preached. Was he still confident in the gospel when incarcerated? Did he really believe 'God works for the good of those who love him' (8:28) after assassination attempts, shipwrecks and snakebites? Could he declare that 'nothing . . . will be able to separate us from the love of God' (8:39) while on death row?

The final verses of Acts record how Paul conducted himself when in Rome. Despite the sense of fear, failure and setback, 'For two whole years . . . Paul proclaimed the kingdom of God and taught about the Lord Jesus Christ – with all boldness and without hindrance.' (Acts 28:30–31).

Paul's confidence in the gospel and his commitment to share it remained constant whatever the circumstances. Despite *his* plans being torn up, Paul was still committed to playing his part in *the onward mission*. While under house arrest in Rome, elite members of the praetorian guard would have been chained to Paul on a rotation basis. Ever the opportunist, Paul considered them to be his 'captive audience' and shared the gospel with them, and with anyone else who visited. Paul also wrote several letters while awaiting sentence – possibly Ephesians, Philippians, Colossians and Philemon.

Today you can visit the dungeon in the Mamertine Prison in Rome, where Paul may have been held at the end of his life. On one occasion, I sat there on my own in the darkness for an hour or so, trying to imagine what it would have been like. 'Scary' was about as far as I got! However, I also noticed a plaque on the wall, which commemorates the fact that several Roman guards were converted to Christianity through Paul's witness. His tireless commitment to mission reminds me of a boxer who gets knocked down but gets up again and fights on – cue the *Rocky* theme tune.

When our plans are disrupted, it's easy to spiral down into a dungeon of despair and to waste precious energy worrying about worst-case scenarios or wallowing in self-pity. However, studying Romans reminds us that God has a plan and is working for good, even when we can't perceive it. The more we meditate on the great truths of Romans, the more resilient we become in the face of setbacks and disappointments. For example, the certainty of God's love in Romans 5 or the sovereignty of God in Romans 8—11.

How about you? Have you found these truths surfacing when circumstances make you feel like you're sinking? The Bible never promises life will be easy. Even when we are on mission for God, we will face some metaphorical storms, shipwrecks and snakebites. But the Scriptures provide a limitless source of encouragement, resilience and hope that keep us buoyant. As Romans 5 promises, tough times develop perseverance and perseverance cultivates hope and 'hope does not put us to shame' (5:5).

> HOPE LIFTS US OUT OF THE RUBBLE OF
> OUR FAILURES, OUR PAIN AND OUR
> FEAR TO RISE ABOVE WHAT AT ONE
> POINT SEEMED INSURMOUNTABLE.
> Erwin McManus[2]

What was Paul's motivation for mission?

In Romans 15, several phrases reveal the motivation that inspired Paul to keep going on mission no matter what. None of them are about increasing his own status, comfort or influence. Instead, listen to what makes Paul tick:

- Verse 6: '. . . so that with one mind and one voice you may glorify the God and Father of our Lord Jesus Christ'.
- Verses 8–9: '. . . so that the promises made to the patriarchs might be confirmed and . . . that the Gentiles might glorify God for his mercy'.
- Verse 17: 'Therefore I glory in Christ Jesus in my service to God.'

In this passage, Paul also cites several Old Testament texts which reveal God's plan to redeem Israel and use them as a light to the surrounding nations. This plan failed because Israel failed to live as God's holy people. However, Paul deliberately picks up on phrases describing Israel's calling and applies them to himself (15:16). As Paul shared the gospel with Gentiles from other nations, he understood himself to be fulfilling the vocation of God's people that stretched right back to Abraham: 'all peoples on earth will be blessed through you' (Gen. 12:3).

Romans 15 therefore provides a rhetorical climax to the whole letter, before the closing greetings in chapter 16. It echoes back to the opening verses, where Paul introduced Jesus as a 'descendant of David' who fulfils what was 'promised beforehand through his prophets in the Holy Scriptures' (1:2–3). Now, in Romans 15, Paul quotes from each section of the Hebrew Bible – the Law, the Prophets and the Writings – to show that when Jews and Gentiles worship together, it bears witness to all creation of what God *has* done in Jesus, *is* doing through the Spirit and *will* do in the end. Now in Rome, as small gatherings of Christians from diverse social and ethnic backgrounds met across the city, they were turning these scriptural promises into a reality. That's why unity, hospitality, welcome and acceptance remain so important for God's people. They are not just nice ideals but an essential part of our mission.

The ultimate goal of the gospel is that God should receive praise from a renewed humanity comprising people from every language and culture. After all, Israel's God 'did not spare his own son, but gave him up for us all' (8:32). The motivation that pulsates through Paul's missionary zeal was therefore that Jews and Gentiles may 'with one mind and one voice . . . glorify the God and Father of our Lord Jesus Christ' (15:6).

Ever since the Tower of Babel, the human race has been

divided. However, through Christ, Paul sees this being reversed as, regardless of race, the gospel reconciles humanity to God and bonds believers into a new community of faith. One of the ways I've experienced the power of this is through bilingual worship. We live in Wales and we regularly gather with Welsh- and English-speaking Christians. Instead of separate meetings, we sing the same songs at the same time but in two different languages. Culturally, there may still be some feelings of animosity, but when we lift up the name of Jesus with one heart and voice, it's a beautiful expression of unity. This is the endgame of mission. When people from every nation worship together, cultural and racial divisions are healed and God is glorified.

What was Paul's method in mission?

Mission comes from a Latin word (*missio*) meaning 'to send'. It alludes to the fact that the gospel involves a double movement. First and foremost, the gospel invites us *in*. Having been justified freely by grace, we 'have peace with God' (Rom. 5:1). Spiritually, we are relocated. Our new status is '*in* Christ' and this enables us to approach God as our Father, secure in the knowledge that we are 'co-heirs' with Jesus. You can't be more *in* than that!

However, the gospel also sends us *out*. The Father commissions us to go into a broken world to share the hope that Jesus has secured. This is what Paul means by 'the priestly duty of proclaiming the gospel of God' (15:16). As priests in the Old Testament mediated the presence of God to those outside, so we are to mediate 'the gospel of God' into every sphere of society. In Jesus' words, we are the light of the world and the salt of the earth (Matt. 5:13–14).

But how do we actually do this? How can we put mission into practice? Let's consider Paul's approach in Romans 15:

I will not venture to speak of anything except what Christ has accomplished through me in leading the Gentiles to obey God by what I have said and done – by the power of signs and wonders, through the power of the Spirit of God. So from Jerusalem all the way around to Illyricum, I have fully proclaimed the gospel of Christ. It has always been my ambition to preach the gospel where Christ was not known, so that I would not be building on someone else's foundation

Romans 15:18–20

Notice Paul's careful phrase in verse 18. He communicated the gospel through: 'what I have said and done'. This highlights a crucial balance for effective mission.

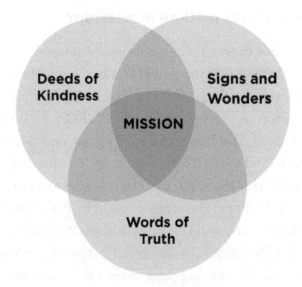

Some of us are more naturally words-oriented. We are confident to share our story, explain the gospel and argue the case. However, our risk is that we rush to speak before we've earned the right to. Out of a concern to win the argument, we may end up losing the person. Others of us will be more deeds-oriented, excelling in acts of kindness and also in supernatural gifts or what Paul refers to as 'signs and wonders'. We are quick to listen, full of compassion and ready to step out in faith. However, our risk is that our kind deeds may not appear to be connected with our faith, or we lack confidence to explain the hope we have in Christ.

Speaking personally, I am more words-oriented. I tend to forget that people are more impacted by what they see than what they hear. One mouth, two ears and all that. So my challenge is to listen more and speak less. How about you? How could you achieve a more effective approach to mission? For me, it really helps to start the day with a simple prayer: 'Lord, show me who I can bless today in Jesus' name.' I find this shifts my focus to showing kindness, generosity and compassion, which in turn means God can open the door for words of truth at the right time.

THIS COMBINATION OF WORDS AND WORKS, THE VERBAL AND THE VISUAL, IS A RECOGNITION THAT HUMAN BEINGS OFTEN LEARN MORE THROUGH THEIR EYES THAN THROUGH THEIR EARS. WORDS EXPLAIN WORKS, BUT WORKS DRAMATIZE WORDS.

John Stott[3]

A few weeks ago, I took my son in our little campervan to play a football match. I managed to park in the perfect spot, right alongside the pitch. Now I could sit inside, make a cup of tea, watch the game and finish writing another chapter of my book on Romans (you're welcome). My plan was working . . . until a big bloke leant against the van and blocked the view! I was about to open the window and ask him to shift, when my own prayer came to mind: 'Who I can bless today?' So I ended up making him a cup of tea instead and we got talking.

Soon after half-time, something unusual happened. I felt the Holy Spirit prompt me to ask, 'Has your heart been broken recently?'

My talkative friend fell silent and filled up with tears. A few months previously, his daughter had suddenly dropped dead from a heart attack. He never even got to say goodbye. Now both of us were blubbing. Once the referee had blown the final whistle, I had a chance to share some hope in Jesus' name. We've since stayed in touch and he always signs off his messages with a broken-heart emoji.

Despite how sophisticated modern society appears, there are so many broken hearts in the world. For our mission to become more effective, Romans 15 can help us bring together three principles, each with a simple question or prompt:

- Verse 18: deeds of kindness – *Who can I bless today?*
- Verse 19: signs and wonders – *What does the Holy Spirit want to say or do?*
- Verse 20: words of truth – *How can I guide this conversation toward Jesus?*

The other principle from Romans 15 is that mission requires a pioneering spirit: 'It has always been my ambition to preach the gospel where Christ was not known' (15:20). In Paul's case, this meant regularly moving to new geographical territories. Next on the list, Spain. Whether he ever got there or not, we don't know. But that's not the point. It's Paul's 'ambition' that challenges us.

In the West, we have assumed for too long that 'mission' means hosting Sunday services or evangelistic courses and praying for more people to turn up. However, in the context of first-century Rome, most people had never heard of Jesus, and Christian gatherings were not permitted. So the believers had to be far more authentic, imaginative and entrepreneurial if the gospel was to infiltrate mainstream culture and impact personal relationships. Now, in the twenty-first century, our situation is not so dissimilar. A whole generation has emerged who know next to nothing about the Bible or Christianity – imagine that. The need of the hour is not church managers but gospel pioneers. Like Paul, we need to discover fresh and creative ways to communicate the unchanging gospel in an ever-changing world.

Notice also that Paul's pioneering initiatives opened up opportunities for others to play their part. In Romans 15 he throws out an invitation to 'join me in my struggle' (15:30). They could do this through financial giving (15:25–7), prayer (15:30–1) or even relocating to travel with him. If you are naturally an entrepreneur with an instinct for making money, starting businesses, designing products and marketing ideas, your talents could help to catalyse new waves of mission. When you channel your 'ambition' toward gospel initiatives, space opens up for others.

So I dare you! Give God permission to disrupt your current plans and invite him to inspire gospel 'ambition' in you. No doubt, what follows will be incredibly challenging, with moments of fear, frustration and apparent failure. However, nothing is more important or rewarding than seeing the gospel transform lives.

In my experience, the only thing better than reaching the summit of a mountain yourself is guiding others there for the first time. The expression on their faces when they take in the view is priceless. While at university, one of my closest friends was Steve. It helped that we both enjoyed climbing mountains, though in other ways we were chalk and cheese. He was a heavy drinker, in and out of relationships, and behind the party smokescreen he struggled with depression. As friends, we occasionally talked about faith. Then, one Sunday out of the blue, Steve came to church and had a powerful experience of God's presence. I remember being shocked as he came up to the front, sank to his knees and sobbed his way into the kingdom. Truth be told, I don't remember much of that night. But I vividly recall our next mountain trip. As we sat on the summit together, I got out the small Bible that I keep in my rucksack, and read a chapter. You guessed it, Romans 8! I don't tend to cry very often, but tears rolled down my cheeks as my best buddy then prayed with me in such an honest, heartfelt way. This is what mission is all about. Sharing hope with friends. What could be more worthwhile? As Paul said, quoting Isaiah, 'How beautiful are the feet of those who bring good news!' (Rom. 10:15).

 REFLECT

Which of these missional practices comes most naturally to you and which are you prone to neglecting? How could you become more intentional about each?

○─○ Part 2: The ground we've covered

READ: Romans 16:25–7

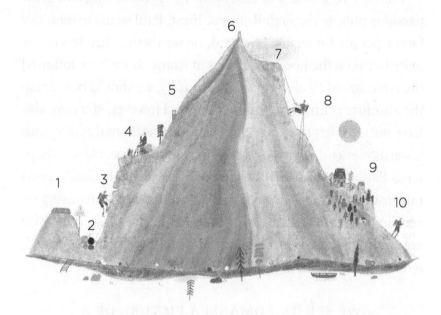

Our adventure through Romans must come to an end. How have you found it? Were you able to navigate the complex landscape or did you get a bit lost? I wonder which section of the route you enjoyed most? Perhaps it was the main ascent from *the valley of sin*, up *the crux of salvation* and along the narrow *ridge of freedom* (Romans 1—7)? Or maybe you enjoyed the panoramic views from *the summit of hope* and glimpsing God's great purpose for Israel as we passed through *the cloud of mystery* (Romans 8—11)? Or perhaps you enjoyed the practical sections on the way down – *the descent of devotion* and *the return to community* (Romans 12—14)? Overall, I hope you are now feeling inspired for *the onward mission* and not nursing too many blisters! As your guide, I want to finish by reflecting on how this adventure might change you for good. How will you live differently on the other side? After all, as Edward Whymper reminded us, the goal is not just to reach the summit but also to return safely, and with good news to share.

You may recall back at basecamp I suggested that two great passions pulsate through Romans. First, Paul wants to mobilise God's people for *mission*. Second, he wants to cultivate greater *unity* between the house churches in Rome. If we have followed the contours of Paul's argument carefully, we should now grasp the absolute centrality of these themes. However, you may also have noticed that the letter does not address them directly until towards the end (Romans 12—16). For the first eleven chapters, Paul explores the height and breadth of God's great purpose as revealed through the gospel. Instead of focusing on certain behaviours, Paul's approach has been to inspire us with a stunning 'view of God's mercy' (12:1). If we grasp this gospel, *mission* and *unity* should then naturally follow.

> WE SEE [IN ROMANS] A PICTURE OF A
> VIBRANT, MULTIFACETED CHURCH AT THE
> HEART OF THE EMPIRE USING THE GIFTS
> AND GRACES OF BOTH MEN AND WOMEN TO
> FURTHER THE SPREAD OF THE GOSPEL.
> Ben Witherington[4]

Having opened Romans with a declaration of confidence – 'I am not ashamed of the gospel' (1:16) – Paul now closes the letter with a prayer, which echoes down through the ages:

> Now to him who is able to establish you in accordance with my gospel, the message I proclaim about Jesus Christ, in keeping with the revelation of the mystery hidden for long ages past, but now revealed and made known through the

prophetic writings by the command of the eternal God, so
that all the Gentiles might come to the obedience that comes
from faith – to the only wise God be glory for ever through
Jesus Christ! Amen.

Romans 16:25–7

The goal of Romans has been to 'establish' Christians in the
gospel. So let's revisit a question we started with. How confident are you in the gospel? Which would you circle now?

1	2	3	4	5
PLAGUED BY DOUBT	VERY UNCERTAIN	UP & DOWN	MOSTLY CONFIDENT	FULLY ASSURED

Without revealing my number, I can honestly say I've moved to
the right as a result of studying Romans and guiding you
through it. Let me share three things in particular that have
struck me about the gospel, which Paul hints at in this closing
prayer.

1. The gospel is a rooted story

Throughout Romans, Paul quotes from and alludes to the Old
Testament in numerous ways. I find this deeply reassuring.
The gospel is not an abstract idea or a new philosophy that a
brilliant mind made up. Instead, it is a story deeply rooted in
history, 'now revealed and made known through the prophetic
writings by the command of the eternal God' (16:26). The
plotline traces all the way back to Abraham (*c*.1800 BC). God
called him into a *covenant* relationship in order that his descendants (Israel) might restore blessing to all *creation*. Where Israel

failed, the Messiah ('a descendant of David' 1:3) has succeeded. Rather like Russian dolls, the 'message . . . about Jesus' (16:25) is therefore nestled inside a much larger story. Why does this increase my confidence? For the same reason being roped to a big boulder reassures me when climbing a challenging route. The tug of the rope around my waist is a reminder that I am now joined to something solid and immovable.

So it is with the gospel. If we are united with Christ by faith, our fragile, vulnerable stories are attached to something deep and immovable. The gospel is underwritten by the faithfulness of God, who will not break his promises even if it means giving up his own Son. So, if this 'God is for us, who can be against us?' (Rom. 8:31–2). Can you feel the tug of the rope? To face life's challenges with confidence, we must be 'established' in this gospel that is as solid as a mountain. The story of our salvation stretches back to *creation* and the *covenant* God made with Abraham and it reaches forward to a *new covenant*, made in the blood of the Messiah, which one day will climax in a glorious *new creation*.

> PAUL'S UNDERSTANDING [OF] THE GOSPEL
> ENCOMPASSES THE COSMOS, THE WHOLE
> OF CREATION — ALL THE WAY OUT AND
> ALL THE WAY DOWN IN HUMAN LIFE.
> Beverly Gaventa[5]

2. The gospel is a relevant story

When Paul refers to 'my gospel' (16:25), it's easy to miss the scale of what he has in mind. The gospel is not just an insurance policy for when we die. While it includes forgiveness of sins, a right standing before God and the Father's love poured into our hearts by the Holy Spirit, the gospel is also good news on a cosmic scale. Jesus was crucified to end the curses of this old creation and raised to life to inaugurate the hope of new creation. His decisive victory therefore heralds hope for the entire planet. As we've seen, the natural environment is currently 'groaning' in sheer anticipation and the Spirit is gathering a new humanity from every nation to bring this hope to fulfilment.

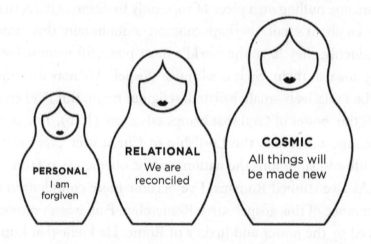

PERSONAL
I am forgiven

RELATIONAL
We are reconciled

COSMIC
All things will be made new

So the message of Jesus is not a private belief but public truth. It is not confined to religious studies lessons or church sermons. In ancient Rome and in our modern culture, the gospel confronts the 'big boys' who want to control the world and fix all the problems. In Paul's day, this meant Caesar and the Empire. In our day it might include expansionist states, Big Tech and political ideologies. The gospel announces that Jesus is Lord of the world, not Caesar or Google. Paul's missionary horizons were therefore enormous: to bring all nations to 'the obedience that comes from faith' (16:26).

Paul opened Romans with this phrase ('the obedience that comes from faith' 1:5), and now he closes the brackets at the other end. What lies between is a message more relevant than we've dared to imagine. 'The obedience of faith' must be lived out in every sphere of life. Think about the topics we've covered: human sexuality (Rom. 1), the natural environment (Rom. 8), revenge culture (Rom. 12), civil authorities, taxes and finance (Rom. 13), race relations (Rom. 14), global mission (Rom. 15). Nothing and no one sits outside the remit of the gospel.

Why might this increase our confidence? Well, imagine someone pulling on a piece of rope only to discover it's actually an elephant's tail (perhaps not on a mountain this time!). Suddenly, they have the world's most powerful mammal staring down at them. So it is with the 'gospel'. We may imagine it to be a relatively small, isolated, religious truth. But Paul knows it is the 'power of God that brings salvation' (1:16). The gospel message announces the Lordship of Christ over every sphere of life and summons the nations to 'the obedience of faith'.

As I've studied Romans, I've become more confident in the relevance of this gospel story. Remember, Paul wasn't remotely fazed by the power and luxury of Rome. He knew that human life will only flourish under the Lordship of Christ. In our affluent and sophisticated culture, we have nothing to be ashamed of. Instead, we are heralds of the one message that can actually deliver on its promises. No amount of technology, science, education or activism can fix what's broken with the world and with you and me. Only Jesus Christ can do that.

3. The gospel is a relational story

Imagine the scene as Phoebe finished reading Paul's letter to a small gathering of Christians in a Roman villa. What happened next? At the risk of being a bit Hollywood, I like to imagine Junia getting up, walking across the room and embracing Herodion. They had been subtly avoiding each other for months, ever since

Herodion questioned whether she should be teaching the Scriptures. I like to imagine Rufus putting away the wine he always brought and pouring a glass of water for Mary. He knew that alcohol caused big problems in her family but was damned if he was going to stop drinking for her . . . that was until Phoebe came with Paul's letter. I like to imagine Aristobulus, the owner of the villa, kissing Nereus and his sister on the forehead and serving them another portion of food. He'd always looked down on his slaves . . . but now he honoured them as guests. The atmosphere in the room was changed because the gospel is a relational story.

If we read the Bible in isolation, we will miss out on its full power. The whole letter of Romans was written to small communities of God's people. Remember the twenty-seven people greeted in Romans 16, several of whom I just mentioned? The mission of God is not just to save individuals but to form a new humanity, united in the Messiah and bound together by the Spirit. The gospel establishes unity, regardless of class, race, gender or any other value-based identity. Remember, 'There is no difference between Jew and Gentile, for *all* have sinned and fall short of the glory of God, and *all* are justified freely by his grace' (Rom. 3:22–4, italics added). We are one family, adopted by our loving heavenly Father. This challenges the tendencies in wider culture to live in ghettoes, to organise around identity politics and to treat those with whom we disagree with contempt. Instead, the gospel is intensely relational. It turns enemies into friends and creates a culture of welcome and inclusion. It challenges us to climb down off our high horse, give up our rights and walk across the room, 'so that with one mind and one voice you may glorify the God and Father of our Lord Jesus Christ' (15:6).

The gospel is more *rooted, relevant* and *relational* than we have dared to imagine. That's why I'm determined not to be ashamed of it. Instead, I resolve to live it out and to share it with others. How about you?

I got up early this morning and drove to the Brecon Beacons near where we live. There's a mountain there which has special significance for me. When my father was battling with cancer, he would struggle up to the top, carrying another rock from a quarry. There on the summit he built a small pile of stones as an Ebenezer (see 1 Samuel 7:12). At least once a month, I head up there to add another rock to the cairn and to find solace in a wild, beautiful place. Today I walked up under moonlight, with the stars glistening overhead. Then I sat on the summit and watched the sunrise. It doesn't matter how many times I've been there; the mountain is always full of surprises. Today, I discovered two soldiers camping near the summit and shared a snippet of the gospel with them.

Whether this was your first time through Romans or it's well-trodden territory for you, this is a mountain that keeps on giving. So don't think, 'I've done it.' The Bible isn't like that. There's always more to explore. God always has more to reveal. Instead, keep revisiting Romans, perhaps using a resource that goes into greater detail next time.[6] Equally, why not use this book to help friends and family explore Romans. After all, you learn even more when you're guiding others.

> YOU CANNOT STAY ON THE SUMMIT FOREVER;
> YOU HAVE TO COME DOWN AGAIN. SO WHY
> BOTHER IN THE FIRST PLACE? JUST THIS . . .
> THERE IS AN ART OF CONDUCTING ONESELF
> IN THE LOWER REGIONS BY THE MEMORY OF
> WHAT ONE SAW HIGHER UP. WHEN ONE CAN NO
> LONGER SEE, ONE CAN AT LEAST STILL KNOW.
> René Daumal, French poet and climber[7]

Above all, may this adventure stay with you back down in the valley of everyday life. May you conduct yourself in the lower regions by the memory of what we've seen higher up. The Bible never promises that following Christ will be easy. Even when we are on mission for God, we will face challenges and setbacks. But the Scriptures provide a limitless source of encouragement, resilience and hope that will keep you going. With that in mind, let me echo Paul's closing prayer over you as you step into *the onward mission*:

> May the God of hope fill you with all joy and peace as you trust in him, so that you may overflow with hope by the power of the Holy Spirit.
>
> *Romans 15:13*

REFLECT: Looking back, what have you most appreciated about our adventure through Romans?

Looking forward, what's your next step on the journey? Share it with someone else and ask them to hold you to it.

> Now to him who is able to establish you in accordance with my gospel . . . to the only wise God be glory forever through Jesus Christ! Amen.
>
> *Romans 16:25, 27*

Notes

Basecamp

1 J. I. Packer, *Knowing God* (Downers Grove: InterVarsity Press, 1993), p. 230.
2 If you're familiar with John Bunyan's classic, *The Pilgrim's Progress*, you will know where I got my inspiration from. Bunyan imagines the Christian life like a landscape with many challenges, which we must navigate.
3 Mary Beard, *SPQR: A History of Ancient Rome* (London: Profile Books, 2015), p. 20.
4 Scot McKnight, *Reading Romans Backwards: A Gospel of Peace in the Midst of Empire* (Waco: Baylor University Press, 2019), Kindle loc. 172.
5 The New International Version is a respected translation, widely used across the English-speaking world and reviewed constantly by a committee of scholars from across the evangelical spectrum. Find out more at biblicaeurope. com/niv-bible (accessed 26 August 2022).

1. The route of the gospel

1 Hien Pham now lives in America and continues to follow Christ and share the gospel with others. For a fuller account of his story, see: www.suffolknewsherald.com/2021/05/21/the-amazing-story-of-hien-pham (accessed 26 August 2022).

2 A phrase used by Professor Phillip Cary in his lecture series 'The History of Christian Theology' (Great Courses, Audible).

3 A reference to the song 'Blinded by Your Grace' by Stormzy, 2017.

4 Queen Elizabeth II, in her Christmas address broadcast to the nation, 2008.

5 McKnight, *Reading Romans Backwards*, loc. 396.

6 John Chrysostom (c.347–407), *Homilies, Romans*, p. 31.

7 The name 'Phoebe' means 'Titaness'. This Greek name suggests she was converted to Christ from a pagan background, as no self- respecting Jewish family would name their daughter after a pagan god/goddess.

8 For example, Paula Gooder's historical novel imagines Phoebe bringing Paul's letter from Corinth to Rome and not only reading it but also explaining it to the house churches. *Phoebe: A Story* (London: Hodder & Stoughton, 2018), esp. chapter 3, pp. 17–22.

9 'Saint Chrysostom: Homilies on the Acts of the Apostles and the Epistle to the Romans', in Philip Schaff (ed.), trans. J. B. Morris, W. H. Simcox and George B. Stevens, vol. 11, *A Select Library of the Nicene and Post-Nicene Fathers of the Christian Church* (New York: Christian Literature Company, 1889), p. 335.

10 In addition, linguistic barriers may have been a challenge, as some were elite Latin speakers but most were Greek speakers with diverse accents.

11 See his brief statement in *Divus Claudius* 25.

12 One procession of defeated Gauls lasted several days. These captives would then end up in the slave markets to replenish the labour force for building Roman roads and other developments.

13 In an interview with Jeremy Paxman: podcasts.apple.com/ za/podcast/tom-holland/id1535105464?i=1000504455398 (accessed 26 August 2022).

14 The Roman Forum was the centre of Roman life, containing government buildings, temples and markets. It was the place for commerce, elections, speeches and triumphal processions.

15 Beverly Roberts Gaventa, *When in Romans: An Invitation to Linger with the Gospel according to Paul* (Grand Rapids: Baker Academic, 2016), p. 46.

16 This analogy draws on a helpful approach developed by Tim Keller in *Romans 1—7 For You: For Reading, for Feeding, for Leading* (Epsom, Surrey: The Good Book Company, 2014).

17 Cited by Timothy Keller, *Romans 1—7 For You*, p. 20.

2. The valley of sin

1 C. S. Lewis, *Mere Christianity* (1952), book 2, chapter 1.

2 *The Office*, Season 1, Episode 6, April 2005.

3 N. T. Wright: *Paul: A Biography* (London: SPCK, 2020), p. 111.

4 John Calvin, *Institutes of the Christian Religion*, translated by Henry Beveridge (London: Clark & Co, 1957), I.11.8.

5 Keller, *Romans 1—7 For You*, p. 27.

6 Thomas Nagel, *The Last Word* (New York: Oxford University Press, 1997), pp. 130–31. The English

philosopher, Aldous Huxley, expressed a similar thought: 'I had motive for not wanting the world to have a meaning; consequently assumed that it had none, and was able without any difficulty to find satisfying reasons for this assumption. The philosopher who finds no meaning in the world is not concerned exclusively with a problem in pure metaphysics, he is also concerned to prove that there is no valid reason why he personally should not do as he wants to do, or why his friends should not seize political power and govern in the way that they find most advantageous to themselves ... For myself, the philosophy of meaninglessness was essentially an instrument of liberation, sexual and political.' Aldous Huxley, *Ends and Means: An Inquiry into the Nature of Ideals* (New York: Harper, 1937), p. 270.

7 Oscar Wilde, *An Ideal Husband*, Act 2.

8 David Foster Wallace, *This is Water: Some Thoughts, Delivered on a Significant Occasion, about Living a Compassionate Life* (New York: Little, Brown and Company, 2009), p. 48.

9 See Tom Holland, *Dominion: The Making of the Western Mind* (London: Little, Brown, 2019), p. 80. In particular, the cult of Aphrodite encouraged sexual immorality. Archaeologists have discovered a detachable phallus and other sex-toys used by prostitutes to worship the gods in orgies.

10 Some have suggested that Paul is only referring here to promiscuous sex and not long-term settled relationships. However, while we cannot draw a direct line between Roman practices and our contemporary culture, it is important to note that, as a well-travelled Roman citizen, Paul would have been familiar with long-term relationships

between same-sex couples. For more on the Roman context of Paul's teaching see Kyle Harper, *From Shame to Sin: The Christian Transformation of Sexual Morality in Late Antiquity* (Cambridge, Mass: Harvard University Press, 2013); Holland, *Dominion*, especially pp. 271–3; N. T. Wright, *Paul for Everyone: Romans Part 1, Chapters 1–8* (London: SPCK, 2014), pp. 19–23.

11 In *Confronting Christianity: 12 Hard Questions for the World's Largest Religion* (Wheaton: Crossway, 2019), Rebecca McLaughlin shares her own experience of same-sex attraction and gives a helpful approach to what the Bible teaches. In *Is God Anti-Gay?* (Epsom, Surrey: The Good Book Company, 2023), Sam Allbery shares his experience of same-sex attraction and how he has understood his identity in response. The organisation *Living Out* also has helpful articles and resources: www.livingout.org (accessed 27 August 2022).

12 Wright, *Paul: A Biography*, p. 218.

13 McKnight, *Reading Romans Backwards*, loc. 2078.

14 Francis Schaeffer, *The Church at the End of the Twentieth Century* (Wheaton, Ill.: Crossway, 1985), pp. 49–50.

15 The need to confess and find release from guilt was powerfully captured by an art project in Brighton train station a few years ago called *The Waiting Wall* (thewaitingwall.com, accessed 27 August 2022). A screen was installed on the concourse by the departures board and commuters could anonymously submit their fears and confessions, which were broadcast for all to see. Some of the things people submitted were quite heartbreaking, but what surprised the artists was that they were inundated with people wanting to get things off their chests and finding it to be a healing process. As Reinhold Niebuhr remarked a

generation ago, no amount of contrary evidence seems to disturb humanity's good opinion of itself. But the evidence is there on every hand in our own period, from the horrors of Auschwitz and a thousand other wartime hells to the killing fields of Cambodia and the wasted millions of Stalin's Gulag, besides the daily toll of gratuitous violence, rape, abuse, abortion, torture and murder in every corner of the globe.

16 Aleksandr Solzhenitsyn, *The Gulag Archipelago* (London: Collins, 1974), p. 28.

17 In *Surprised by Joy*, C. S. Lewis defines chronological snobbery as 'the uncritical acceptance of the intellectual climate common to our own age and the assumption that whatever has gone out of date is on that account discredited' (San Diego: Harcourt, 1966), pp. 207–8.

18 Alcoholics Anonymous, 'The 12 Steps of AA', alcoholics-anonymous.org.uk/About-AA/The-12-Steps-of-AA (accessed 27 August 2022).

19 Tom Holland, Twitter, 27 October 2021, twitter.com/holland_tom/status/1453640072247529475 (accessed 27 August 2022).

3. The crux of salvation

1 See Romans 6:22; 7:6; 1 Corinthians 15:20; Ephesians 2:13; Colossians 1:22.

2 Leon Morris, *The Epistle to the Romans* (Leicester: IVP, 1988), p. 173.

3 This incident is cited in Philip Yancey, *What's So Amazing About Grace?* (Grand Rapids: Zondervan, 1997), p. 45.

4 Cited from the 1998 film edition of *Les Misérables*, 2012, directed by Tom Hooper.

5 D. A. Carson, *The Difficult Doctrine of the Love of God* (Wheaton, Ill.: Crossway Books, 2000), 70.

6 Cited in Nicky Gumbel, *The Bible in One Year: A Commentary* (London: Hodder & Stoughton, 2019), p. 139.

7 N. T. Wright and Michael F. Bird, *The New Testament in its World: An Introduction to the History, Literature and Theology of the First Christians* (London: SPCK, 2019), p. 517.

8 Gratitude is a deep human emotion that people feel it whether or not they believe there's a God. See Emma Green, 'Gratitude Without God', *The Atlantic*, 26 November 2014, www.theatlantic.com/health/archive/2014/11/the-phenomenology-of-gratitude/383174 (accessed 27 August 2022).

9 John Stott, *The Message of Romans: God's Good News for the World* (Leicester: IVP, 1994), p. 134.

4. The place of peace

1 McKnight, *Reading Romans Backwards*, loc. 2667.

2 Wright, *Paul for Everyone: Romans Part 1*, p. 83.

3 In Wesley's journal, 24 May 1738.

5. The ridge of freedom

1 See related article: Ed Thomas, 'Burnley's Pastor Mick – from dangerous drug dealer to lifesaver', BBC News, 18 December 2020: www.bbc.co.uk/news/stories-55273677 (accessed 27 August 2022). Mick's new book tells his story in greater detail. Mick Fleming, *Blown Away: From Drug Dealer to Life Bringer* (London: SPCK, 2022).

2 I can't help wondering if Paul's strong reaction is in part because he has been tempted by this illicit thought himself. He despises it so intensely because he knows it undermines the work of grace in our lives. God's eternal purpose is that we should be 'conformed to the image of his Son' (Rom. 8:29).

3 In particular, the statement, 'I am unspiritual, sold as a slave to sin' (7:14) conflicts with what Paul says about Christians in Romans 6, where he declares that they have been freed from sin.

4 In ancient rhetoric, a writer or speaker could impersonate the argument of somebody else (known as a speech-in-character), whether a real person or fictional character. If this is what Paul is doing in Romans 7, then 6:1—7:6 and 8:1–17 form brackets around 7:7–25 and thereby reveal what those who are in Christ Jesus and who share in the Spirit have been delivered from. i.e., cycles of defeat and despair.

5 This verse has several variations but the one cited here is attributed to John Berridge. See Jason Meyer, *The End of the Law: Mosaic covenant in Pauline Theology* (Nashville: B&H, 2010), p. 2.

6 Martyn Lloyd-Jones, *Romans Chapter 6 sermon* (1989), cited in Tim Keller, *Romans 1—7 For You*, p. 144.

7 This idea is conveyed in a prayer by Augustine in his *Soliloquies* (Book 1, 1.2–4).

6. The summit of hope

1 Stott, *The Message of Romans*, 217.

2 Wright and Bird, *The New Testament in Its World*, p. 519.

3 In a letter dated 17 June 1 BC, a Roman soldier called

Hilarion writes to his wife who is expecting a child. In a throwaway line he says, 'Above all, if you bear a child and it is male, let it be; if it is a female, cast it out.' Cited in John Dickson, *Bullies and Saints: An Honest Look at the Good and Evil of Christian History* (Grand Rapids: Zondervan, 2021), p. 35.

4 Paul is primarily conveying who we are 'in Christ'. So, rather than this being a gendered statement, it is a more generic fact. God has only one eternal Son. So if we are 'in him', we share in his sonship by the Spirit. From a theological perspective, this does not refer to his masculine identity so much as his eternal relationship with the Father. So 'sonship' is our status 'in Christ', whether we are male or female.

5 See Tom Holland's interview, 'Christ and his endless resurrections', The Pull Request, 20 August 2021: www.thepull-request.com/p/christ-and-his-endless-resurrections-09a (accessed 8 September 2022).

6 John Calvin, *Institutes* 2:4.17.2.

7 Aldo Leopold, *A Sand County Almanac: And Sketches Here and There* (Oxford: Oxford University Press, 1949), p. 165.

8 In Allen Goddard, 'A Rocha International: Championing Christian Hope in the Environmental Crisis', p. 5. atyourservice.arocha.org/wp-content/uploads/2016/08/christian-hope-environmental-crisis.pdf (accessed 30 August 2022). For more on biblical motivations for creation care and other helpful resources visit A Rocha's website www.arocha.org/en (accessed 30 August 2022).

9 J. I. Packer, *Keep in Step with the Spirit* (Leicester: IVP, 1999), p. 129.

10 Tim Keller, *Romans 8—16 For You* (The Good Book Company, 2015), p. 52.

11 Cited in Keller, *Romans 8—16 For You*, p. 55.

7. The cloud of mystery

1 In AD 1290, all Jews were expelled from England until the seventeenth century, echoing Claudius' first-century edict.

2 Billy Graham used this illustration in a sermon he preached on Matthew 7 in Anaheim, California, in 1969.

3 Equally, in Romans 9 Paul affirms that salvation extends beyond Israel when he quotes Hosea: 'I will call them "my people" who are not my people; and I will call her "my loved one" who is not my loved one' (9:25).

4 McKnight, *Reading Romans Backwards*, loc. 1271.

5 C. H. Spurgeon, 'Divine Sovereignty'. A sermon delivered 4 May 1856 (London).

6 You can watch the conversation here: 'Why the Bible makes sense of modern life • Tom Holland & Andrew Ollerton', YouTube, 30 April 2021: www.youtube.com/watch?v=f2_W6eCijV4 (accessed 30 August 2022).

7 Not to mention the persecution of Jews within the Byzantine Empire, under Islamic rule and within the Ottoman Empire. The persistence of Jewish people even as a diaspora is remarkable given their more powerful ancient neighbours, whether Canaanites, Hittites or Amorites, have long since disappeared.

8 Israel was not chosen because of superior morals, nor does God's purpose for them rely upon their actions. The story of Israel is ultimately one of God's faithfulness in spite of his people's failure.

9 See William Ramsay, *The New Testament Scholar*, cited in Keller, *Romans 8—16 For You*, p. 85.

10 The positive expression of this in the Old Testament is that several non-Jewish characters such as Rahab and Ruth

were incorporated into the covenant people because they chose to worship Israel's God and shared in their blessing.

11 See the 'I Met Messiah!' webpage for some personal stories: www.oneforisrael.org/met-messiah-jewish-testimonies (accessed 30 August 2022).

12 A trend in modern interreligious dialogue between Jews and Christians is to insist that Israel can be saved through its covenantal arrangement under the Torah. However, Paul is adamant that if salvation can come through the law, 'Christ died for nothing' (Gal. 2:21), and he believes that Christ is the end or goal of the Torah: 'so that there may be righteousness for everyone who believes' (Rom. 10:4).

13 In a sermon, Augustine used the Latin phrase *'Si comprehendis, non est Deus'*. Sermon 117 in *Patrologia Latina*, Vol. 38, pp. 661–71.

14 There are also pottery inscriptions, *papyri* (ancient paper), and *ostraca* (limestone notepads) which state, 'Nero is Lord', or even proclaim him 'Lord of the entire world'. We could compare ancient sculptures to modern-day advertising campaigns and ancient coins to social media feeds that are passed on through many transactions in homes, marketplaces and temples. The people passing them on would not even realise they are participating in political and religious propaganda.

15 Stott, *The Message of Romans*, pp. 283, 285.

8. The descent of devotion

1 See Tom Wright, 'Women Bishops: It's about the Bible, not progress – Tom Wright – UPDATED & Retort', VirtueOnline, 23 November 2012: virtueonline.org/women-bishops-its-about-bible-not-progress-tom-wright-updated-retort (accessed 30 August 2022).

2 C. H. Spurgeon, *All-Round Ministry* (Edinburgh: Banner of Truth, 1981), p. 230.

3 Though the source of this quote is uncertain, it has been attributed to Ralph Waldo Emerson.

4 Wright and Bird, *The New Testament and Its World*, p. 522.

5 In Norman Grubb, *C. T. Studd: Cricketer and Pioneer* (Fort Washington: Christian Literature Crusade publications, 1933), p. 28.

6 Michael F. Bird, *Romans: The Story of God Bible Commentary* (Grand Rapids: Zondervan Academic, 2016), loc. 11669.

7 Tertullian, *Apologeticus*, ch. 39, sect. 7, italics added.

8 Miroslav Volf, *Exclusion and Embrace: A Theological Exploration of Reconciliation* (Nashville: Abingdon Press, 1996), pp. 291–2.

9 Queen Elizabeth II, in her Christmas address broadcast to the nation, 2014.

10 This quote comes from King's famous sermon, *Loving Your Enemies*, preached in Washington DC on Easter Sunday 1958.

9. The return to community

1 Equally, in the Old Testament, Israel was a distinct nation with governors, taxes and laws. However, their exile to Babylon brought an end to this. Even after returning to their homeland, they experienced a series of occupations, culminating in the Roman invasion of Palestine in 63 BC. This only strengthened the expectation that the Messiah would be a military leader, who would liberate Israel from foreign occupation so they could be a nation once again-This explains why Jesus was such a disappointment. Instead

of attacking the Romans, he made a whip and turned on the temple. Instead of liberating Israel, he was crucified by their archenemy.

2 This is sometimes referred to as Constantinianism as it began to be an issue from the fourth century onwards when the Roman emperor, Constantine, converted to Christianity. He went on to host a significant gathering of church leaders known as the Council of Nicea (AD 325) in order to settle theological disputes. This approach has resurfaced in a modern movement known as 'Dominion' theology, which seeks to justify the establishment of political nations governed by Christians and ruled under a form of biblical law.

3 The denarius was a Tiberian tribute penny which had on one side an 'image' of Tiberius' bust with an inscription that read, 'Son of the divine Augustus'; then on the other side it said, 'High priest', accompanied by a depiction of Tiberius' mother Livia posing as the goddess Roma.

4 Douglas J. Moo, *The Letter to the Romans* (Grand Rapids: Eerdmans, 1996), p. 809. As Scot McKnight notes, Paul's affirmation here is also subversive: 'Paul says it is the God of the Bible, not the Roman gods and emperors, who ordains government. Above the Roman "governing authorities," then, are not the gods of Rome but the God of the crucified, raised, and ruling Messiah – King Jesus'. McKnight, *Reading Romans Backwards*, loc. 1010.

5 Cited in Bird, *Romans: Story of God Commentary*, loc. 12067. Origen had experienced Roman brutality first-hand.

6 Esau McCaulley, *Reading While Black: African American Biblical Interpretation as an Exercise in Hope* (Downers Grove: IVP, 2020).

7 McCaulley, *Reading While Black*, p. 342.

8 Catherine Clinton, *Harriet Tubman: The Road to Freedom* (New York: Little, Brown, 2004).

9 Sarah Hopkins Bradford, *Scenes in the Life of Harriet Tubman* (New York: W. J. Moses, 1869), pp. 20, 22.

10 Attributed to a speech given in 1985.

11 This story of Von Roenne is told briefly in Ben McIntyre's book *Operation Mincemeat* (New York: Bloomsbury, 2016), which has now been made into a film.

12 Cited in Bird, *Romans: Story of God Commentary*, loc. 12515.

13 Keller, *Romans 8—16 For You*, p. 142.

14 McCaulley, *Reading While Black*, p. 106.

15 Cited in Phillip Staff, *History of the Christian Church* Vol. 7 (W. M. Eerdmans, 1910), pp. 650–3.

16 Stott, *The Message of Romans*, p. 358.

10. The onward mission

1 In Edward Whymper's book, *Ascent of the Matterhorn* (London: John Murray, 1879), p. 298.

2 Erwin McManus, *Soul Cravings* (Thomas Nelson, 2008), p. 2.

3 Stott, *The Message of Romans*, pp. 380–1.

4 Ben Witherington, *Women and the Genesis of Christianity* (Cambridge: Cambridge University Press, 1990), p. 189.

5 Gaventa, *When in Romans*, p. 46.

6 I recommend the following: N. T. Wright, *Paul For Everyone: Romans Part 1 and Part 2* (London: SPCK, 2014); Scot McKnight, *Reading Romans Backwards: A Gospel of Peace in the Midst of Empire* (Waco: Baylor University Press, 2019); Tim Keller, *Romans 1—7 For You*

and *Romans 8—16 For You* (Epsom, Surrey: The Good Book Company, 2014; 2015).

7 René Daumal *Mountain Analogue: A Novel of Symbolically Authentic Non-Euclidean Adventures in Mountain Climbing* (London: Gerald Duckworth & co.,1952).

MORE FROM
ANDREW OLLERTON

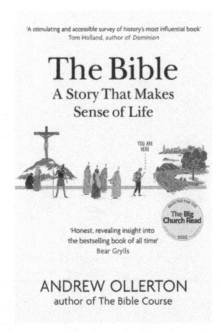

When we make sense of the Bible, the Bible makes sense of us.

'Honest, revealing insight into the bestselling book of all time.'
Bear Grylls

'A stimulating and accessible survey of history's most influential book.'
Tom Holland, historian and author of *Dominion*

OUT NOW | 9781529327014 | £10.99

Explore the letter to the Romans

Using the stunning backdrop of Rome, Andrew Ollerton presents an inspiring and insightful course exploring Paul's letter to the Romans. Containing ten videos and a participants guide, The Romans Course will take you on a deeper journey, helping you discover your place in God's story.

Visit biblesociety.org.uk/theromanscourse

Dr Andrew Oller[...]

The Bible Course

Although the Bible is the world's bestselling book, there are still many of us who find it to be big and intimidating.

But it needn't be that way.

Using a unique storyline, this eight-session course shows how the key events, books and characters all fit together.

You'll get to see the BIG picture and discover how the Bible applies to your life.

Visit biblesociety.org.uk/thebiblecourse